ALTERNATIVE FUTURES FOR WORSHIP
Leadership Ministry in Community

ALTERNATIVE FUTURES
FOR WORSHIP
Volume 6
Leadership Ministry in Community

Volume Editor

MICHAEL A. COWAN

Authors

JAMES D. WHITEHEAD
EVELYN EATON WHITEHEAD
DAVID N. POWER, O.M.I.
JOHN SHEA

THE LITURGICAL PRESS
Collegeville, Minnesota 56321

Cover design by Mary Jo Pauly

Manufactured in the United States of America.

ISBN 0-8146-1498-1

1   2   3   4   5   6   7   8

Library of Congress Cataloging-in-Publication Data
Alternative futures for worship.

Includes bibliographies.
Contents: v. 1. General Introduction / volume editor,
Regis A. Duffy ; authors, Michael A. Cowan, Paul J.
Philibert, Edward J. Kilmartin — v. 2. Baptism and
confirmation / edited by Mark Searle ; by Andrew D.
Thompson . . . [et al.] — v. 3. The eucharist / edited
by Bernard J. Lee ; by Thomas Richstatter . . . [et al.]
— [etc.]
    1. Sacraments (Liturgy) 2. Catholic Church—Liturgy.
I. Lee, Bernard J., 1932–
BX2200.A49   1987   265   86-27300
ISBN 0-8146-1491-4 (set)

CONTENTS

RITUALS

THE CONTRIBUTORS

MICHAEL A. COWAN is adjunct professor of pastoral theology in the school of theology of St. John's University in Collegeville and in the school of divinity of The College of St. Thomas in St. Paul. He is co-author (with Bernard J. Lee) of *Dangerous Memories: House Churches and Our American Story.*

JAMES D. WHITEHEAD is a pastoral theologian and historian of religion. He serves as consultant in education and ministry through Whitehead Associates, South Bend, Indiana, and is a member of the associate faculty of the Institute of Pastoral Studies at Loyola University, Chicago.

EVELYN EATON WHITEHEAD, a social scientist, is consultant in eduation and ministry through Whitehead Associates, South Bend, Indiana, and a member of the associate faculty of the Institute of Pastoral Studies at Loyola University, Chicago.

DAVID N. POWER, O.M.I., is professor of systematic theology and liturgy in the department of theology at The Catholic University of America, where he currently is chair of that department.

JOHN SHEA is chair of the systematic department and director of the doctor of ministry program at Mundelein Seminary. His latest work is *The Spirit Master* (Thomas More Press, 1987).

PREFACE

Alternative Futures for Worship is not a product. It is rather a window through which a relationship may be observed. Or to change the image, it is a listening device with which a conversation may be overheard. The participants are sacramental theology, liturgical experience, and the human sciences.

All of life—like all the world—has the possibility of mediating the transformative encounter between God and human history. That is its sacramental character. In the Roman Catholic tradition there has evolved over a long history a system of seven sacraments. These are not our only sacramental experiences. But they occupy a privileged sacramental role in the life of this Christian community.

Each sacrament concerns itself with the religious meanings of some important slice of human life. There are not many slices of life whose patterns and interpreted meanings have not been probed and described by the human sciences. It is crucial, therefore, that sacramental and liturgical theology pay very careful attention indeed to the deliverances of the human sciences. Religious experience cannot, of course, be reduced to the descriptive reports of the human sciences. Yet it would be foolhardy to theologize or "liturgize" apart from serious consideration of these many empirical attempts to understand the character of lived experience in our culture and our time.

Each volume in this series exemplifies the processes of encounter between sacrament, liturgy, and the human sciences: what reports from the human sciences are being considered; how do these understandings affect the meaning structure of the sacrament; how would these meanings find liturgical expression. Every volume in the series has this fundamental agenda, but each takes it up in its own particular way. Our aims are modest; we have not intended to produce any exactly right conclusion. We only care to engage in serious, imaginative, and highly responsible conversation.

It may seem that proposing alternative sacramental rituals is irresponsible, and it would be if they were proposed for anyone's actual use. They are not! This is not an underground sacramentary. We are most aware of the tentative and groping character of each of these attempts.

However, we believe with William James that the best way to understand what something means (like this conversation between Christian experience and the human sciences) is to see what difference it makes. James says you must set an idea to work in the stream of experience to know what it means. We choose ritual as that stream of experience.

Sacramental rituals are not themselves the sacraments. The sacraments are temporally thick slices of life which through time mediate religious experience. The liturgical rite is but one moment in this thicker-than-rite sacramentalization of life. It is a privileged moment though. Ritual is a moment of high value if it illuminates and intensifies the meaning of sacrament. Leonard Bernstein's "Mass for Theatre" speaks movingly of the absurdity of ritual when it has lost touch with the lives of the people who are supposed to be celebrating it. When private meanings and public ritual meanings do not intersect (which is not to say coincide), the absurdity is thundering.

Because a ritual puts a sacramental understanding under the spotlight, we have elected to explore the conversation between sacramental life and the human sciences by imagining ritual appropriations of the fruits of the conversation. That is our way of setting an idea to work imaginatively in the stream of experience. That, and nothing more! But that is a lot.

We suggest that any readers of this volume who have not done so read the introductory volume. There we have tried to say more fully what we think we are about in this entire series and why the many authors who contributed to it are convinced that this project is a quite right thing to do. We are happy to have you listen in on our conversation. Our long-term hope is that you may join it.

Bernard J. Lee, S.M.
San Antonio, Texas

FOREWORD:
GLIMPSES OF THE CONTEMPORARY SITUATION

Peter Gibbons is the administrator of a large, urban parish. Married and the parent of three children, he is a member of the parish ministry team which includes a pastor and two other priests, three women religious, and four lay ministers. When he took this position four years ago, both Peter and the other ministers saw his job as restricted to the financial management of the parish. Since then an increasing sense of shared leadership in the parish has led to his participation in other aspects of the community's ministry. Gradually his job has become a ministry and his career a vocation.

Personally Peter is coming to a different and more powerful sense of his role in the parish. He is reading in theology and finding himself concerned with more than the financial aspects of the parish's mission statement. He also has formed a support group of other lay parish administrators in his area. It began as a very "professional" group, but the members find they are giving less time to the sharing of management techniques and more attention to the religious and theological aspects of their vocations.

Acknowledged as one of the four or five leaders in the parish, Peter continues to muse about how best to define his relationship to the ordained ministers in the parish.

Christina Samuels and Kay Forte are two women religious serving Catholics in a small town in northern Michigan. The church has had no pastor for the past three years due to the lack of priests in this diocese. A priest does visit every other Saturday evening to celebrate the sacraments. Six months ago the bishop appointed these two sisters to be "the representatives of the Church and its ministry" in this town.

With backgrounds in social work, the two women began ministries of healing and counseling, ranging from helping troubled marriages to clearing up Social Security problems for some elderly members of the community. An initial, mild resistance to these women ministers—"Don't we even deserve a priest?"—has given way to a delight in the amount of attention suddenly available: the two ministers are available every day; they reside in the community; and there are even *two* of them!

After some hesitation the two women began to gather the community for prayer: Scripture reading and a homily would accompany the sharing of the Lord's Body provided by the biweekly Eucharist. Designated as the official representatives of the Church in this small community, the women have become its ordinary liturgical leaders.

What are the possibilities and limits of this emerging leadership? How might the community understand the leadership of their new pastors?

A congregation of sisters is gathered at their headquarters for two weeks in mid-August, for retreat, theological reflection, and rest. The congregation is small, less than three hundred. During most of the year, the sisters live in groups of two or three persons, frequently at some distance from the motherhouse as well as from others in the congregation. The time together each summer is an important part of the life of the congregation as a whole. It reenforces the sense of belonging and rekindles the awareness of shared mission. The summer experience culminates in a mission-sending ceremony on the final Sunday, as most of the sisters return to their ministries.

When the ceremony was initiated in the mid-1960's, it took the shape of a blessing offered to each sister at the end of Mass by the priest who was chaplain of the motherhouse community. In recent years the liturgy committee within the congregation has become more involved in the design of the ceremony and of the Eucharistic liturgy in which it takes place. Members of the congregation have become more active in the readings and prayers, and those in congregational leadership now assume roles in blessing and commissioning the sisters.

When Father Sanders, longtime chaplain and much loved friend of the congregation, died in 1980, the sisters were informed that the diocese would no longer be able to assign a priest as resident chaplain. It proved difficult for them to make other arrangements for daily Eucharist at the motherhouse, a development that was especially disappointing for the infirm sisters in residence there. At this point a number of the sisters who live at the motherhouse year-round decided to worship regularly at the local parishes in which they were involved in various ways. The liturgy committee, in discussion with the sisters in the infirmary, designed Communion services that are conducted there regularly; efforts are also made to invite priests to celebrate weekday Mass in the infirmary with some frequency. An additional responsibility of the liturgy committee has become to arrange with one of the priests in the local area for the celebration of the Sunday Eucharist at the motherhouse once a month and on special community occasions.

Several days prior to the mission-sending celebration this August, the chair of the liturgy committee learned that the priest scheduled as celebrant for the commissioning liturgy was unable to attend. She called the committee together to discuss alternatives. Several suggestions emerged. One was to begin calling priests in the area, in the hope that one might be able to clear his schedule, even on such short notice. A second recommendation was to approach one of the local parishes where the sisters are well-known, with the request that the ceremony be held there after one of the regular Sunday liturgies. A third possibility was to keep the celebration at the motherhouse, but to redesign it so that it was no longer part of the Eucharist. None of these options generated much enthusiasm. Each presented practical problems, but the committee members found difficulties with the theological presuppositions of each of these options to be even more troublesome.

Gradually consensus emerged: "Surely we have within this community the resources we need to celebrate the Lord's presence among us, as we take leave of one another to continue our ministry in his name." With this conviction the committee approached the members of the congregation's leadership team to invite their participation in presiding at the proclamation of the Word, the offering of thanks, the breaking of the bread, and the sharing of the cup.

The bishop in a medium-sized diocese in the West has a special concern. The number of priests in the diocese is small—especially by the standards of dioceses in other parts of the country—and shrinking. The median age of the clergy is rising, as fewer young men are ordained for ministry in the diocese.

The morale of the priests seems low. Most live alone. This has been a regular pattern of rectory life here, but now it is even more the case. Declining numbers have meant that there are few parishes that can enjoy the presence of more than one priest. Many of the clergy feel (and are) overburdened. The expansion of parishes, coupled with a burgeoning of diocesan level agencies, has meant that most priests hold more than one set of "full-time" responsibilities. The diocese is no longer experiencing large numbers of resignations from the priesthood, but the signs of psychological stress among the clergy are obvious—loss of savor in their ministry, apathy, depression, alcoholism, and other physical complaints.

Yet in many ways the diocese is flourishing. There is a new energy alive in the local Church. The Catholic population in the area is growing. Several new parishes have been established recently and more are planned. Over the past decade the diocese has benefitted from an influx of talented and trained personnel, most of them lay persons and religious who function in staff positions in many diocesan offices and agencies, and, increasingly, in parishes as well. The level of competence and commitment that characterizes these professionals in the ministry of the diocese is of great consolation to the bishop. He senses, though, that their presence and increasing prominence in the diocese is a part of the morale problem among his priests.

A recent diocesan-wide program of parish renewal was a great success. In most parishes a significant number of parishioners participated in the year-long program, and many are eager to continue their new level of involvement in the life of the Church. The bishop, at first surprised and then gratified by the response in the parishes, is now concerned about how best this new enthusisasm is to be nurtured and put to use. Many pastors, he knows, are even more concerned. Some fear that, if not tended well, the energy of the renewal effort will quickly fade. Others are afraid that it will not fade! Their fear is that it will generate a host of additional projects and committees to add to their already overcrowded list of parochial responsibilities.

Thus the bishop's dilemma. He feels a special responsibility to the priests. Ministry to them, as well as with them, is an important part of his understanding of his own role. And he knows that without their support his own ministry in the diocese becomes very difficult. But his ministry goes beyond just the priests. And he is genuinely enlivened by those developments that signal new directions in the diocese, even as he realizes these are precisely the developments that generate the greatest ambivalence among the priests. He is badgered by women religious and lay persons in ministry who find that the priests with whom they are working, often under whom they are working, are the chief obstacle to their ministry.

The bishop's challenge, as he sees it, is to be able to respond, at both the practical and the procedural levels, to this wealth that is emerging in forms of new ministry in the community of faith, while supporting and celebrating the important ministry of his priests.

In a small, rudely constructed shelter in the middle of a Latin American barrio, there were about thirty adults seated in a circle on rough chairs or wooden boxes, with small children amusing themselves in a corner, or running in and out of the door, or clinging to their mothers. There was a Bible open in front of the people, and they were discussing the text that would be heard at next Sunday's liturgy. They were relating this text to two of their own struggles: first, to have proper drains installed in their district; second, to provide the means for a young girl to get medical treatment for a serious illness. As the evening proceeded, the group took up the request of a couple who wanted to have their child baptized, in order to make a decision about how this request should be met. It was clear throughout the meeting that some members took more initiative in explaining the Bible, others in outlining the community's action on the two issues discussed, and others in interspersing the meeting with song and music or other moments of prayer. There was also one relatively silent member of the group who, it gradually became apparent, was chairing the meeting and giving some form to the agenda. Later a missionary spoke of the various responsibilities assumed by this community and of the increasing need to organize seminars and instructions for the leaders, so as to enable them to keep abreast of their task. He also spoke of the suspicion in which civil and military authorities held such groups and of the quality of witness and fidelity required of their members.

A church compound on the outskirts of an Asian city, consisting of a courtyard, the hall that did for a church, a store, and some offices, was filled with fifty-three families who were temporarily dwelling there while fighting the commune for squatting rights in the area. Again there was discussion, report on action taken, Bible reading, poetry, and prayer. It was also obvious that these people were being led a song and dance by civil and military authorities and that they needed firmer and better informed leadership were they to come to grips with the true nature of their struggle.

Basic communities, whether in harmony with bishops or whether in a situation of conflict over the role of the Christian in social and political development, by their very nature raise the issue of ordination as one concerning the relation between the people and those who have power. From their existence the role of the charismatic gifts and of popular discernment as a foundation for structural development becomes clearer. So do the issues about mission in the world and service to the poor that Christian communities and their leadership have to face. Given their recognition by other churches and a freedom to develop internally, these communities can become communities of believing people who by faith and hope change the nature of the Church's presence in society. They can show how issues of ecclesial power affect the power that the Church as a people has in economic, social, political, and cultural developments. The internal organization of a Church and its place in society are related intimately to one another.

Most Catholic parishes have a large and "hard to pin down" membership. The majority of the members are regular Sunday churchgoers, but they are relatively quiet and go unnoticed in the crowd. They become visible to the full-time ministers only at significant moments. They enter the world of the minister at times when they are soaring (birth, weddings, anniversaries) or crashing (sickness, divorce, death). When these people become the focus of ministerial activity, it is usually a question of creating a religious context for a major event of their life. The minister is called upon to construct a "sacred canopy" under which the life-joy or life-struggle can go on. These people express no need for an explicit Christian community nor do they jump at the chance to join the various small group movements of the parish. Their community needs are met by family and friendship groups. They are religious people who pray and struggle with the moral life. They go to church, but they are not "into" Church.

Catholicism is a mass religion. The local Church may be a community, or better, a community of communities, but it is also a place that multitudes of people have been trained to think of as their personal contact point with the divine. Therefore, at those times when they think they should be in touch with God, they are going to gravitate toward the Church and call upon the ministers with their needs. This may not be the ideal of Church participation or the fantasied situation of ministerial dreams, but it is part of the reality of large urban and suburban parishes. It does not seem that it is going to go away in the immediate future.

Once the needs are taken care of, the relationship with the minister will be less involved. Any intensity that was generated during the time of need will lessen. Casual friendliness will take its place. Over a period of time the minister will get to know many people and inevitably will become the confidant of the secrets that are revealed in times of joy and sadness. Ministry in this environment is individualistic, serial, and, to those involved in it, seemingly endless in its demands.

In most parishes there is a lot going on. In one parish, Parish Sunday consists of passing out forms at all the Masses. There are sixty-four organizations listed on the forms. The parishioners are asked to sign up on the basis of what they would be interested in that would help them develop their faith and in what area they would like to be of service to the community. A small sampling of choices would be: teaching catechetics, visiting the sick, volunteering to take an unwed mother into one's home, Bible study groups, senior citizen service, days of recollection, and soup kitchen duty. In this atmosphere whenever a need arises, an organization to minister to it is not far behind.

In any given parish there will be those who say the rosary at Mass and those who sneer at those who say the rosary at Mass. There will be women in jeans who are dedicated to the soup kitchen and who do not understand the high-heeled women of the Women's Club who are excited about a guest speaker on macrame. There will be a CUF contingent sniffing for heresy and a Call For Action group demanding financial accountability. The people in religious education will claim the liturgy team is subverting their best efforts. There will be people who want to know in every waking moment, "what the Church really teaches," and those who say, "I don't pay any attention to what the Church teaches, but it's a nice place to belong." Pluralism is the air the parish breathes.

In this setting ministry becomes, in the fashionable phrase, coordinating the gifts of the faithful. The minister is continually working with small groups who are trying to serve some larger target population. In this sense they are forming a ministerial congregation, a community which is conscious of needs and conflicts and

skilled in organizing to meet those needs and address those conflicts. In this highly charged and complex environment ministry must
also be visionary and reconciling. There is a need for a theological
vision which can include the diversity and deal with the tension
of differences. Some people in ministry may be of a prophetic bent,
speaking the truth as they see it and watching who scatters and who
gathers. But most ministers are of a reconciling bent. They want
to keep people talking to one another. Somehow they feel the cir-
cus tent is big enough for all.

Church architects seem to be letting more sun in. Church build-
ings were once stained glass heavens. The only sun that managed
to come in arrived filtered through multicolored mosaics of Christ
or a saint. This darkened the interior of the church and made it
into a separate world, obviously more sacred than the outside. But
in many churches today there is a combination of stained glass and
clear windows. Often the stained glass sections are behind the altar and the clear glass section along the side or in the ceiling. It seems
to be saying that this is a sacred place, but so is the world outside.
We do not leave the world by entering this church. We bring it in
with us, and we see it differently. We do not block out the sun which
lights the everyday world. Its rays will warm our sacred place.

This image suggests an important aspect of the life-setting of
the minister. Large parishes which are part of large institutions tend
to create their own needs and then minister to them. They specify
membership requirements, and then ministries are created to help
people meet those requirements. In this way a parish becomes a
self-contained reality. It relates to people only in terms of the needs
it has created in them through its declaration of demands. People
begin to talk about "church life" and "real life." The parish does
not intersect the "real life" of people but continues to try to promote its concerns and priorities as of real importance. Religion and
Church take on an air of unreality. The stained glass windows have
blocked out too much sun.

In this life-setting, ministry is trying to find a balance between
being environment-creative and environment-reflective. A parish
will always provide a distinct environment, because its explicit task
is to place people in worshipful contact with the divine. But it should
not be an escape environment. It should reflect the concerns and
questions of the environments it interacts with. The Church is not
a separate world but an interpretation and orientation within the
only world there is. As such, ministry finds its home in the real

life conflicts of people. This means that a parish is built on the immediate issues of work and family and through those issues on the larger concerns of culture and society. Much of ministry is the attempt to discern the sacred in the secular and run with it. The clear glass lets the sunlight in, but it also allows ministers and people to look out.

INTRODUCTION:
LEADERSHIP IN THE COMMUNITY OF JESUS CHRIST TODAY

Michael A. Cowan

Something of the diversity and vitality of emerging leadership in the community of Jesus Christ is captured in the preceding vignettes. The chapters in this volume constitute a conversation about leadership, power, and ministry in the contemporary Christian community—a conversation whose partners include Christian tradition, social psychological theory and research, the developmental psychology of adulthood, and liturgical and pastoral theology.

The flow of our conversation is as follows. In James Whitehead's chapter entitled, "Christian Images of Community: Power and Leadership," the two metaphors of hierarchy and mutuality which are in contention in today's Church are explored. It is in the light and shadow of these traditional images that we struggle today for a reenvisioning of the conditions of emergence and ritual celebration of authentic Christian leadership.

Evelyn Eaton Whitehead's chapter, "Leadership and Power: A View from the Social Sciences," is the next and pivotal moment in the conversation. I say pivotal because Evelyn Whitehead has offered her fellow authors and readers an empirical description of contemporary cultural and religious images of power, of the social processes involved in leadership, of stages in the life of a group, of the role of designated or official leaders, and finally of the experience of personal power in leadership. In her chapter we have a concrete description of groups, leadership, and power. These phenomena and their interrelationships *are* the reality on which this volume is to reflect theologically and pastorally. Whitehead describes the everyday acts of leadership in groups which, when put in a particular religious context, could become the embodiment of servant leadership in the Christian community.

What follows next are two theological reflections on the empirical reality described in Evelyn Whitehead's chapter. In "Stewardship: The Disciple Becomes a Leader" James Whitehead draws on the psychology of adult development in the tradition of Erik Erikson to illuminate the maturing process entailed in the development of all Christians from discipleship to stewardship. In "Liturgy and Empowerment" David Power explores the necessary canonization of power within religious settings, especially as this is reflected in liturgical practice. He shows how liturgical celebration shapes and is shaped by the understanding and practice of power, and he sharply identifies the problematic in our contemporary situation in that regard.

The final reflective chapter of the volume, John Shea's "Theological Assumptions and Ministerial Style," relates the foregoing social, scientific, and theological reflection on leadership and power to ministerial practice. Shea first examines ways of identifying the "operative theology" of ministers, then describes three sources of ministers' theological visions, and ends with an exploration of the faith convictions and theological understandings which energize ministerial styles. In Shea's reflections the pastoral fruit of the preceding conversation is gathered.

The final moment of our conversation with each other and with you involves the presentation of several rituals. These rituals are our shared imaginings of ways that Christian communities might ritually celebrate the emergence of the authentically servant leadership which is, or ought to be, its hallmark. For a community to partake of such rituals is for it to shape and be shaped by an image of the leader as servant.

"Conversation" is more than a metaphor for the structure of this volume, which began and continues as a lively conversation among those involved. One incarnation of that dialogue is captured in the text before you. We hope that it will both join with and provoke further conversation and action among those concerned with justice and love in the unavoidable exercise of leadership and power within the Christian community. The give-and-take of authentic mutual conversations lies at the heart of servant leadership.

1. CHRISTIAN IMAGES OF COMMUNITY:
POWER AND LEADERSHIP

James D. Whitehead

Our understanding of leadership is always shaped by our images of power and our visions of community. Is leadership an individual possession, or an aspect of group life? Does the power associated with leadership belong to individuals, or is it part of a community's self-possession and maturity? This chapter examines how Christian convictions about leadership, and its power, arise from the visions and metaphors of our shared life.

Our expectations of Christian leadership are rooted in our images of who we are and how we are together. The interplay of various ecclesial self-images in our religious history is extraordinarily rich and complex. We have imagined ourselves as a pilgrim people, as members of a kingdom, as a family. These images carry within themselves implied visions of leadership and power. Pilgrims follow a guide, a more experienced companion of the journey; a kingdom is governed by a ruler; a family follows its parents. As we explore the future of Christian leadership, what shall be the interplay of these and other inherited visions? Will these cherished images admit new visions to this interplay? What will be the prevailing shape of the ministry of leadership in future communities of faith—parent, king, guide, or some shape only now tentatively imagined?

When we explore the influence of our visions of community life on our beliefs about leadership, we do well to be aware of the theology of power that supports our differing visions. Christian reflection, whether on leadership or community, begins with convictions about God's powerful presence among us. Where does this power come from and what shape does it take in our group? How is it recognized in our leaders? How do our images of a shared life suggest the distribution of God's power in different gifts, vocations, authorities? To reflect on leadership is to necessarily examine the question of power, God's and ours.

Two images of Christian community contend with one another in today's Church. These are hierarchy and mutuality. As metaphors they suggest our shared life, rather than being exact descriptions of it. By examining them as two models of Christian community, we will be able to clarify our changing convictions about leadership and power.

Hierarchy: Community, Leadership, and Power

Less than twenty-five years ago the prevailing image of Christian community, of who we were as a people, was that of a hierarchy. This image or model of the Church held many implications for the style of leadership expected in a Christian community. In this corporate self-image we pictured ourselves arrayed together in a vertical fashion, occupying different strata in a pyramid. The pope guided bishops who led priests who, in turn, administered to communities of lay Christians. A graphic reminder of the vertical character of this self-image can be found in the "Constitution on the Church" from the Second Vatican Council. It describes this hierarchy with a quote from St. Augustine: "from the bishops down to the last member of the laity . . ." (*Lumen Gentium*, #12). If this hierarchical image of Christian life at times felt too regimented, it is important to recall that it was an image of belonging: this is how we were together, how we loved one another. A great advantage of this self-image was its clarity: we knew where we stood. Laity, clergy, and vowed religious each knew their role and what to expect of each other in this stable Christian world. Whence did this image arise?

In the first generations of Christian life, the followers of Jesus Christ were gradually forming images of their life together. They remembered Jesus' informal gathering of others around him; they recalled his insistence that they serve one another rather than seek privileged status or superiority. But against this informal intimacy of believers stood a powerful religious and cultural model of community life. Their own Jewish heritage was one of kings and priests, leaders of privileged position in a hierarchically structured community. The fledgling Christian community was also part of the Mediterranean culture that envisioned reality, whether it be cosmic, political, or religious, as a hierarchy. What could be more natural? The Roman Empire displayed an effective model of hierarchical government, and soon the expanding Church was complementing its convictions about its members' equality in Christ and its servant leadership with the vertical structure of a hierarchy.

The image of a hierarchy was more than a model for the structuring of a community. A metaphor of community always includes images of power—where this group gets its authority, who is in charge. In a faith community understood as a hierarchy, power tends to be envisioned as descending. From a transcendent God power is handed down to the pope and other bishops, thence to priests, and finally to the laity. Given by God, in whom all power resides, the power of ministry and administration is mediated by the clergy to the laity. The power of leadership to celebrate the sacraments and to make decisions for the community "belongs" to the office or role of the clergy rather than the community. Power, in a vertical metaphor of community, is necessarily pictured as "power over," jeopardizing Christian memories of Jesus' power as also a "power for" and "power with." Those at the bottom of the hierarchy tend to be imagined as receiving power; the laity become consumers of power, rather than generators and sharers.

From the beginning the administrative austerity of this self-image was softened by complementing it with the imagery of a family. The top rung of this hierarchy was occupied not by a king or chairman of the board but by a leader who was called "Holy Father." Laity were not merely the bottom rung of this hierarchy like slaves but were affectionately called "the children of God" and were led by priests who bore the title of "Father."

The compelling quality of this self-image began to wane as Christians, clergy and laity alike, became more aware of some of its limits and dangers. Any image, of course, has special strengths and specific weaknesses. It is graceful as it illumines God's presence among us, but because of its very specificity (God is present in *this* way), it is always in danger of also concealing other aspects of this presence which is ultimately unimaginable. The weakness that began to be perceived in this hierarchical image of our life together was its implications for ministry and leadership; both were imagined in a descending fashion. In a hierarchical Church leaders are both elevated above the community and necessarily reach down to care for it. In the many centuries when the largely uneducated faithful felt content to picture themselves as a flock cared for by shepherds and as children ministered to by parents, this ecclesial self-image remained most graceful. As the faithful changed, both in education and in a sense of what adult faith entailed, this hierarchical image began to seem less graceful. We began to see more clearly the temptation built into such a model of Church and ministry: descending care easily becomes condescending. This is not because the Church's ministers were unholy but because to envision ministry as reaching down invites us to imagine the minister as superior. Christian theology and spirituality have fought this temptation, reminding ministers that such structural superiority is not one of holiness. But religious rhetoric, such as naming our leaders "Reverend" and "Your Eminence," often overcame our other efforts.

The temptation that seemed endemic to a hierarchical image of the Church and ministry often led to paternalism. There can be great delight in imagining God's care as paternal; calling God "father," as Jesus instructed us, we invest this unseen presence with the affection and protection often experienced in the human family. A special danger arises when we apply this title to our leaders. Both the father of a family and the head of a parish are tempted to allow paternal care to slip into paternalistic control. Paternalism, in the family and the parish, is care become constraint; when "father knows best" in a way that excludes discussion and negotiation, bonds of affection bend into bonds of restraint. In a paternalistic context followers are not only seen as children, but are made to feel like children.

Paternalism illumines another implication of a hierarchical self-image: the distance between the leader and the community. In a hierarchical image of the Church, the leader is separated from the community in the role of mediator between God and the community. This aspect of mediator, an important and enduring part of leadership, became increasingly emphasized in Christian history until the priest/leader found himself significantly removed from the community he served. In the following pages I will try to trace this separation of leadership and power from the Christian community.

Coalescing of Ministries

The historical movement toward the envisioning of the Christian leader as a hierarchical mediator, complex as it is, may be glimpsed in a two-stage development during the first five centuries of the Christian tradition. The first development we might call a coalescing of ministries. In the first generations of followers of Jesus Christ, communities appeared to be composed of various ministries, both enthusiastic and disorganized. After Pentecost the first Christians found themselves gifted with different charisms or abilities to heal, preach, administer, and prophesy.

During the next two centuries, however, a double dynamic impelled a change in this experience of diverse powers in the community. Christian groups were growing in the many regions around the Mediterranean, and at the same time these communities were confronted with differing interpretations of Jesus' message. The need to both organize a rapidly expanding Church and to preserve this fragile new faith from heresy and misinterpretation eventually led to the coalescing of the various ministries of teaching, healing, prophesying, and liturgical presiding into the single ministry of the presbyter/bishop. Gradually the variety of ministries in a single community were absorbed into the role of the community leader. This was most often a bishop, who was still a local pastor during the second century, assisted by presbyters or elders, who often functioned as a kind of parish council.

For a time deacons were active members of this leadership constellation, acting as delegates of the pastor in handling, for example, a community's practical questions of health care and finances. One of the most interesting stories, still to be fully understood, concerns the gradual disappearance of the ministry of prophecy. Clearly a distinct and vibrant ministry in the earliest communities, this function was often carried out by itinerant preachers who called people to conversion. This was the ministry of John the Baptist and of the itinerant Jesus wandering about Galilee. During the second and third centuries these prophets gradually disappeared as a recognizable group of ministers. The activity of prophecy would survive in various muted forms—for example, in mystics and later, in religious orders; officially it was absorbed into the ministry of the presbyter and bishop. To collapse the function of the prophet, who is a challenger of the status quo, into the role of the official community leader, who is necessarily charged with the preservation of the group, is to jeopardize an important and useful tension in the community.

The first movements toward a hierarchical Church are seen, of course, in this coalescing of ministries. The whole range of ministries once found in splendid confusion through the community gradually became the province of the bishop who delegated some of them to presbyters who, in turn, ministered to increasingly passive communities. The community leader was becoming *the* minister in the community. Eventually this minister would be expected to act as teacher, healer, administrator, and prophet for a community that otherwise seemed to lack these gifts and services. From an earlier time when power seemed to be dispersed throughout the community in various gifts, power coalesced into the unique leadership of the presbyter/bishop.

Before turning to the second development that more dramatically determined the future of Christian leadership, it is useful to recall the common shape of such a community in the second and third centuries. A faith community was commonly led by a bishop, usually a married man chosen by the community. He was assisted by and accountable to presbyters, a small group of community members notably matured in their own faith. Such a community was emphatically a lay community; no distinction had yet arisen between clergy and laity. Bishops were known by the secular title of "overseer," and presbyters by the name of "elder." There was as yet very little talk of community leadership under the sacred title of "priest." Liturgical leadership followed from one's practical role as community leader.

Presbyters Become Priests

Between the third and fifth centuries the second development in the evolution of hierarchy in the Church occurred: presbyters became priests. This phrase encapsulates a complex metamorphosis of Christian leadership from a community function to a priestly status. As Christian communities grew and reproduced themselves during the fourth century, bishops gradually gave up their roles as local pastors to become regional administrators. Into their places as community leaders stepped presbyters, but these were now presbyters-become-priests.

An enthusiasm during this time for the Jewish imagery of the high priesthood encouraged Christians to describe their leaders as priests, that is, cultic officials like those who had served in the temple of Jerusalem before its destruction. The various leadership functions of the "elder" were increasingly subordinated to his cultic and liturgical role as "priest." Two very practical influences on the future shape of community leadership ensued.

First, the cultic purity of the leader, now envisioned as a priest in charge of the community's sacred rites, began to receive special attention. The Synod of Carthage in 390 stated that married community leaders-become-priests were to abstain from sexual intercourse with their wives; this abstinence was related to their role at the sacrifice of the Mass. Gradually celibacy replaced such abstinence as an ordinary expectation, if often unmet, of this community leadership. At the Second Lateran Council in 1139, celibacy was finally and officially promulgated as a requirement for community leadership/priesthood. In this discussion of leadership, celibacy as an important Christian life style is not under review; this gift, disengaged from an unchristian rejection of the body, has continuously demonstrated its gracefulness and fruitfulness in Christian history. Here the question is the bonding of this specific life style to the ministry of community leadership. This bonding occurred in our history out of a developing sense of the role of the community leader and the Eucharist in Christian life. As our sense of this ministry and this sacrament continues to develop, we may anticipate a separation of the role of community leader from a specific life style.

Second, during this same period there arose an inclination, inherited from Roman society, to distinguish professional ministers from the body of the faithful. "The clergy" as a distinct social class now appeared in society. The social difference would soon be emphasized by the adoption of distinctive garb. That this development was resisted by the Church itself is witnessed in Pope Celestine's urging in 428 against such distinctive attire, since a bishop should be distinguishable from his flock "by his teaching, not his dress."

An earlier coalescing of ministries into the single ministry of the community leader was now being complemented by a separation of the leader from the community. Socially distinct as a member of the clergy, the leader was also separated by his life style of celibacy. And the fruit of these important changes was evidenced in liturgical shifts: the table of the Eucharist meal became the altar for the Holy Sacrifice of the Mass. Both vocabulary and architecture changed. With the Mass now the cultic province of the priest, it gradually became less a question of "a community celebrating the Eucharist," and more that of "a priest saying Mass." And the altar began to move from its more central location in the church toward one end of the building. Before long a curtain would be installed between the sanctuary and the main body of the church to be closed during the most sacred part of the liturgy. Visually separated from the Eucharist, the faithful would then be described as "hearing Mass." Another custom that arose from the sixth century was the private Mass. A growing intimacy between the priest and the Eucharist was matched by a growing distance between a community and the Eucharist. Not only was the community leader/priest more and more separated from the community, he was taking the Eucharist with him.

The development of the priesthood over the following centuries and its tensions with community leadership form a most complex story. Two shifts in the medieval Church's vision of priesthood merit mention because of their influence on contemporary Christian life. First, in the Lateran Councils of 1179 and 1215 the priestly ministry was firmly defined in terms of its liturgical role. The celebration of the Eucharist and the other sacraments was a "power" enjoyed by this ministry, apart from considerations of community. Thus was overturned, unintentionally but effectively, the prohibition by the Council of Chalcedon in 451 of "absolute ordination," the commissioning of a person to leadership apart from any community. A theology of ministry, now focused on the liturgical role of the priest, became almost divorced from a theology of community. Communities of believers were now imagined to be lacking the ability and right to celebrate the Eucharist; this "power" and the leadership it implied were the prerogative of the priesthood.

Second, in a powerful movement of piety generated by the Gregorian Reform of the eleventh century, priesthood became emphasized as a devotional state of life, apart from its function of community leadership. Monks, until then laymen, began to be ordained in order to partake of this pious state. Gradually abbeys and religious orders filled with monks and brothers now ordained as priests, but who in no way were involved in the exercise of community leadership. The anomaly of this divorce of the priestly role from the community leader's function is vividly evident today. A large Catholic university, for example, may house dozens of priests who exercise valuable ministries of teaching and administration, but in no way act as community leaders. Efforts are made on weekends to distribute this ministerial wealth to parishes that are otherwise lacking in liturgical leadership. This and other anomalies of contemporary ministry compel us to reexamine the connections among power, community, and leadership.

Mutuality: Community, Leadership, and Power

As John Kenneth Galbraith has observed in *The New Industrial State*, a hierarchical model of a group and its leadership rarely exists in its pure form:

> Power is assumed to pass down from the pinnacle. Those at the top give orders; those below relay them on, or respond. This happens, but only in very simple organizations—the peacetime drill of the national guard or a troop of boy scouts moving out on Saturday manoeuvres. Elsewhere the decision will require information. Some power will then pass to the person or persons who have this information.[1]

Power arises from many sources—even in a hierarchy.

In the Christian tradition the hierarchical vision of Church, with its implications for leadership, has always contested with and been complemented by another powerful image of shared life. In the Second Vatican Council the Church began to reemphasize an image of community that was as ancient as that of hierarchy; this was the image of a radical mutuality. The roots of such an idealistic image lay in the early Church's sense of unity and equality in Jesus Christ. As proclaimed in Paul's famous statement in his letter to the Galatians, when followers of Jesus are baptized, they enter a way of life that knows no distinction of class, privilege, or status:

> All baptized in Christ, you have all clothed yourselves in Christ, and there are no more distinctions between Jew and Greek, slave and free, male and female, but all of you are one in Christ Jesus. (Gal 3:27-28)

In a contemporary Church so clearly divided by distinctions of clergy and lay, women and men, such a vision may sound like little more than a remnant of a group's beginnings. Yet since the Second Vatican Council, this sentence has emerged from Paul's letter like a long-buried prophecy.

The council itself displayed a new mood of mutuality in its leadership. Bishops met for many months with the pope in a collegial fashion. We began to recall that the pope was both the unique head of the Church and *one of* its leaders. *Primus inter pares*, first among equals, again began to describe, if tentatively and with many retreats, this ideal of Christian leadership.

And this image of collegiality spread beyond the hierarchical leadership. Parish councils began to appear; communities became enthused about the possibility of shared decision-making and leadership. Communities of vowed religious, so significant in the implementing of the council's hopes, began to reimagine themselves. From a severely hierarchical self-image, in which the leader was expected to mediate God's will to the members of the community, these groups began to envision discernment and decision-making not as descending from the leader to the group but as arising from the community itself. Such an altered vision invited a more collegial exercise of leadership and community discernment.

This enthusiastically recovered image of mutuality was, like that of a hierarchy, an image of belonging. But unlike the vertical image of a hierarchy where members find themselves at different ranks and levels, this new self-understanding was one of horizontal belonging. We began to picture ourselves *beside* each other instead of above and below. In the accompanying liturgical reform our celebration of the Eucharist was changing in the same direction of greater mutuality. Reversing the transition of the fourth and fifth centuries, we began to speak of the Eucharist as a shared meal instead of the Mass as a Sacrifice. The altar was both turned around and brought toward the center of the church. Shared decision-making began to affect the Eucharist as it became more thoroughly community-planned and celebrated. This enthusiasm for the Eucharist was, of course, at times contradictory: even as it became more of a community event, restrictions were reaffirmed against girls as acolytes and women as liturgical leaders. Mixed signals abound as we move between conflicting images of who we are.

As the imagery of mutuality spread through Christian communities, team ministry began to flourish. We were surprised to find so many gifted individuals in the parish. Where had they been—these people so capable at caring for the ill, at planning, at managing finances? Suddenly Paul's picture of the Christian community had a very contemporary feel. The teachers of Paul's communities were now working with the youth and in premarriage ministry in our parishes; the healers of his Corinth were now hospital chaplains or were establishing hospice programs; the administrators of Paul's communities were now bringing a more accountable bookkeeping to the parish; the prophets of Corinth were now on the parish council, asking difficult questions about social justice and community priorities; those with "the gift of faith" in the Pauline community were now seen to be those seasoned Catholics who, having endured every kind of crisis and loss, anchored the parish's ability to keep the faith.

In this experience of renewal, new images of power were released. A community was the scene of a variety of strengths and gifts; God's power was moving visibly among us. This power seemed to *belong* in the community, instead of depending on being delivered by official ministers of the Church. Our differences in power and weakness bound us together rather than separating us as superiors and inferiors. Communities, stirred by this experience of power, began to recover a sense of agency and potency. They were more than needy groups of laity; they had something to give. They were called to be generators of faith and grace and not just consumers.

Such a reenvisioning of our shared life would lead us inevitably to different expectations about leadership. In an earlier, more hierarchical image we had pictured the leader as mediator, the one through whom God's gifts and grace came to the community. Such an image of leadership tended to portray the leader as standing apart, different from other believers by reason of this specialized, more sacred role. When we imagine ourselves in a more mutual fashion, we expect the leader to be found *among* us, rather than above us. We invite our leaders to be a more intimate part of the community. From this new position the leader is recognized as one of the ministers of the community. Holy like us, the leader is also wounded like us. Welcoming the leader back into its midst, the community asks this minister to be less a mediator and more a coordinator of its many gifts and ministries.

In this new role the community leader supports and guides the various ministries of the community rather than supplying them. Karl Rahner describes the priest/leader as having

the function of guiding and maintaining in unity all other functions and their holders, constituting and sustaining a Christian community as Church, functions which, of course, cannot really belong exclusively to any single individual.[2]

Once the various ministries of the earliest Christian communities had coalesced into the presiding priest/leader, an enormous burden was laid on that leader; he became healer, preacher, administrator, prophet, and liturgical presider. In a hierarchical image of the Church, relief from this unhappy burden was most often sought by delegating different responsibilities: the pastor would distribute and share various ministerial tasks, tasks which belong essentially to his priesthood.

In the image of mutuality recalled in the Second Vatican Council, believers came to be recognized as gifted for ministry not by

delegation from the community leader but from the Spirit—the giver
of gifts—blowing where it would. The leader's role began to be envisioned less as mediating and more as ancillary: the leader stands
alongside other ministers, orchestrating a power already present in
the group. "Ancillary" does not mean peripheral or unimportant.
Its religious nuance comes from Jesus' mother, who was "the hand-
maiden (*ancilla*) of the lord," and reminds us that Christian leadership is more service than command, ministering to power rather
than providing it.

The virtues specific to this role of servant leadership are the abilities to coordinate—thus the necessary skills of communication and
conflict resolution—and to celebrate—thus the required grace of
public presence and presiding. This can be either an energizing or
demeaning shift in the vision of Christian leadership. It is energizing if one is stirred by an intimate association with other gifted members of the community, but demeaning if leadership is interpreted
exclusively in images of priestly mediator and ruler.

As the role of community leader becomes more functional as
coordinator of ministries and less cultic as the sole celebrator of
the Sacrifice of the Mass, vocabulary necessarily changes. The leader
is described less in terms of "molding and ruling" (surprisingly, still
the imagery of the Second Vatican Council's "Constitution on the
Church"), and more in Rahner's vocabulary of "guiding and maintaining." Reverend and father seem less appropriate titles within
the collegial images of mutuality; brother and sister better capture
the ancillary and servant role of the leader in this different vision
of the community, and presbyter, as signifying maturity in faith,
replaces the more cultic title of priest.

From Hierarchy to Mutuality

This shift from a more hierarchical vision of community and
leadership toward a more mutual self-understanding has been, to
put it mildly, uneven. Instead of a graceful glide from one model
of the Church to another, we often experience this transition more
as a hesitant shuffle. In this transition our rhetoric has raced ahead
of our structures and of our ability to implement change. We talk
of collegiality and shared leadership, but dioceses most often recognize the parish priest as the only genuine leader. Women religious
are encouraged to fully share the ministry of hospital chaplaincy,
except for its sacramental ministries of reconciliation and the Eucharist. This ecclesial shift leaves us split among ourselves as we

make this transition with different speeds and enthusiasm. Within a single ministerial team there are likely to be very different expectations about decision-making. As a member of the team, you expect collaboration to be total, from reflection to decision; as the designated leader I look forward to the team's input on a decision that is essentially mine.

Caught in the midst of such a powerful shift, a transformation in our vision of community and leadership, it is helpful to recall that this is not a change from bad to good; it does not demand a repudiation of our past. It does not require an either-or choice but is rather a move along a continuum. Both images of our communal life are equally ancient; both appear in the Second Vatican Council's "Constitution on the Church"; both images will certainly be part of our future as a people. These images, after all, are grounded in a dual conviction of God's transcendence and immanence. Jesus Christ mediates to us a God that is unimaginably beyond us; the Spirit makes the same God present within our community in a manner more intimate than we could hope.

The ministry of community leadership will always include elements of distance and unity. Leaders must, at times, stand apart from the community, either to challenge it or to represent to a local group the larger Church's hopes or demands. And leaders must also belong within the community as servants, identified with the people in their faith and sinfulness, and not just representatives of a distant power.

Christian communities and Christian leadership will always combine the images of hierarchy and mutuality. When we question these images about "which is right," we must expect the Zen-like answer: yes. Failure in our common life and in ministry happens when we flee to the extremes of this continuum. At the tyrannical extreme of a hierarchical interpretation, the local pastor appears as the sole and unaccountable ruler; he alone is thought to possess the power to lead, though he may paternalistically delegate some of his authority. At the romantic extreme of a mutuality vision, there appears the nightmare of endless committee meetings in pursuit of total consensus.

Finally, we may wonder how the ideals of hierarchy and mutuality fit the rhythm of the Church's historical maturing. Musing on Evelyn Eaton Whitehead's delineation of the stages of a group's maturing (presented in the next chapter), we may guess that perhaps a hierarchical and paternal orientation toward leadership fit the earliest stage of the Church's growth. Care and control mingle in this stage of growth; a group looks outside itself to leaders who seem different and stronger for their guidance. The children of God, still in their infancy, cling to strong and caring parents.

Only as the Church matured, did the adult ideal of mutuality become a realistic possibility. This image of our shared life, always part of our heritage, awaited the gradual seasoning of Christian communities. In the new season of religious maturity since the Second Vatican Council, we are becoming more comfortable with our diverse powers and gifts. Power among us is recognized not just in its vertical dimension as "power over" but also in its lateral, mutual dimensions of "power with" and "power for." In this mood of mutuality, the power of the leader becomes reenvisioned not as a personal possession but as a community power attributed on a "guest basis" to some of the group's ministers.

This shake-up of power and the shift from a hierarchical toward a mutuality model of life together have us confused. In such a painful transition it may help to recall Paul's image of creative but painful change: "We know that the whole creation has been groaning in travail until now" (Rom 8:22). If groaning is a sign of pain, of limbs grown stiff from lack of movement, it is also a sign of life. The Body of Christ is groaning today, but not because it is dying. It groans in its experience of new vitality and in its efforts to move more gracefully into the future.

Footnotes

1. John Kenneth Galbraith, *The New Industrial State* (Boston: Houghton, Mifflin, 1967).

2. Karl Rahner, *Theological Investigations*, vol. xix (New York: Crossroad, 1983) 75.

References

Congar, Yves. "The Historical Development of Authority in the Church. Points for Christian Reflection," ed. John M. Todd. *Problems of Authority*, Baltimore: Helicon, 1962, pages 119–153. A brief and excellent overview of authority in the Catholic tradition, especially in relation to ecclesiology and ministry.

Fiorenza, Elisabeth Schüssler. *In Memory of Her, A Feminist Theological Reconstruction of Christian Origins*. New York: Crossroad, 1983. In this forceful and evocative recovery of the origins of Christian ministry, the author uncovers the role of women and an early "discipleship of equals." This is a difficult but very rewarding book.

Käsemann, Ernst. "Ministry and Community in the New Testament," in his *Essays on New Testament Themes*. Philadelphia: Fortress Press, 1982. In this classic, and just reissued, essay a highly respected Protestant theologian makes some telling points on the early development of Christian ministry.

Mitchell, Nathan. *Mission and Ministry: History and Theology in the Sacrament of Order*. Wilmington, Delaware: Glazier Press, 1982. An excellent review of the growth of Christian ministry in the early Church and the subsequent development of a theology and spirituality of priesthood. A well-written and honest examination of both the past and present of the priestly ministry.

O'Meara, Thomas Franklin. *Theology of Ministry*. New York: Paulist, 1983. In this "cultural history of ministry," the author traces the "metamorphoses" of Christian ministry as the Church responds to changing cultural contexts and needs. An excellent book with full and useful notes.

Schillebeeckx, Edward. *Ministry: Leadership in the Community of Jesus Christ*. New York: Crossroad, 1981. This extraordinary book addresses a variety of questions crucial for contemporary ministry, especially the relation of ministry to the community, the medieval development of the "power" of the priest, and celibacy. Schillebeeckx continues his examination of Christian history and community in *The Church with a Human Face*. New York: Crossroad, 1985.

Schütz, John Howard. *Paul and Apostolic Authority*. Cambridge: Cambridge University Press, 1975. A good, contemporary study of authority as the interpretation of power.

Whitehead, James D., and Evelyn Eaton. *The Emerging Laity. Returning Leadership to the Community of Faith*. New York: Doubleday, 1986. This book offers a full examination of leadership in the Church today. Chapters 9–10 offer a fuller exploration of the historical dynamics discussed in this chapter.

Whitehead, Evelyn Eaton, and James D. *Seasons of Strength*. New York: Doubleday, Image, 1986. In Part One the authors trace the maturing of a Christian vocation through the stages of child, disciple, and steward.

2. LEADERSHIP AND POWER:
A VIEW FROM THE SOCIAL SCIENCES

Evelyn Eaton Whitehead

As a community of faith, our experience of leadership has undergone a dramatic shift over the past quarter century. Over this period there has also been a significant transformation in the way that leadership is understood in the social sciences. How leadership emerges in a group, the ways that persons in roles of designated leadership influence the processes of group life, the relationship between leadership style and group effectiveness—there are new explanations today, based on a broader appreciation of what goes on among us in groups.

This chapter will examine several elements of this new understanding of leadership, especially as these help to illumine the shift we have experienced in the purpose and practice of religious leadership. We begin with an examination of images of power that influence our expectations. The discussion moves to an analysis of the social processes involved in leadership and then to a description of the dynamics of leadership in the group setting. We turn next to the role of the designated leader and the experience of personal power in that role. There is a final summary statement of learnings for the community of faith.

I. Images of Power

The images of power shared within a group help define its leadership. Part of a shared social consciousness, these images most often function implicitly, providing many of the "givens" we accept without question as we begin to explore alternatives for leadership in the community of faith. It is useful to bring these images to explicit awareness, for only then can they be evaluated. And it is only through a process of evaluation that we can determine the degree to which these images express our own best hopes and deepest convictions and the degree to which they serve more simply as blinders, preventing us from seeing more adequate shapes of leadership that are emerging. Here we will explore two sets of images that influence, and to that degree limit, how leadership is experienced among American Catholics today. The first set dominates the broad cultural imagination of most Americans; the second set is more directly relevant to our shared history as Catholic Christians.

CULTURAL IMAGES OF THE LEADER

In his provocative work *Authority*, social psychologist Richard Sennett points to two dominant but deficient images that define leadership in Western culture today. The first of these is the paternal leader, who offers to care for us if we will but accept the price of (benign) control. This is an image of leadership in which both power and maturity belong to the leader alone. The paternal leader wants to use these resources for the group, but only according to the leader's idea of what is best and only so long as the group recognizes and accepts its own impotence. There is no mutuality here. The group needs the leader, since the leader alone is imaged to have power; the leader needs the group to reinforce this image of unequal power. But the reciprocity of social power is denied.

The image of paternalism is static, with fixed categories of the powerful leader and the powerless group. The leader does not exercise authority in order to nurture the group's power but to substitute for it. The emergence of power within the group is interpreted as ingratitude ("what more do you want from me") or betrayal ("after all I have done for you"). Paternalism is a leadership of false love: where genuine love wants the continued growth of the beloved, paternalism wants continued dependence. This image of the leader, which confounds care and control, influences the patterns of authority in many institutional settings today. But perhaps nowhere are the limits of paternalism being experienced as keenly and challenged on as many fronts as in the community of faith.

A second image that complicates our efforts to develop more adequate structures of leadership in the community of faith today is the autonomous leader. If paternalism is a mode of control that "cares" too much, autonomy is a mode of control that does not care. Here the leader is imaged as the disinterested expert. Possessed of the resources of special competence or needed expertise, the leader-as-expert exercises this power in the group, but asks nothing in return. At first glance, this can seem a liberating image of leadership. There are "no strings attached" to the power that the expert offers to the group. To those who know too well the strings that bind the group to a paternal leader, the image of the expert can seem a welcome alternative. But here again, the reciprocity of social power is denied. The group needs the power of the expert, while the expert has no need of the group. The image reflected is again that of unilateral power. In addition to the power of needed competence, the expert has the power of self-sufficiency. The emotional message, "there is nothing I need from you," is most often interpreted as "you possess nothing of power or worth on your own."

In paternalism the implicit social equation is "you need me to care for you; I need you to be grateful." In autonomy it is "you need my expertise; I do not need you at all." Both these images are distortions; each seeks to establish an understanding of social power that denies mutuality. In each the process of power is one-way. In both paternalism and autonomy it is the leader who has power and choice. It is up to the leader to decide when and if and how to give this power to the group. In both these images of leadership, the group stands without the power that it needs; power is outside the group. The group may be fortunate enough to benefit from the power of a leader. If so, it may make a return of gratitude but, lacking as it is in power, it has nothing else to give. Even its gratitude is seen as less a choice than an expectation. For the group to ask more of its relationship to the leader is impertinence. Besides, it will lead only to frustration. The group has nothing the leader wants or needs. Its single stance is receptivity, as the leader's single stance is power.

The static quality of these two images is even more damaging. Neither expects a growth in the power of the group or the development of a relationship where the giving and receiving can go both ways. Each of these images of leadership claims that the current categories of leader and led are permanent. Each predicts that any questioning of this status quo, the balance of the social power among us, can result only in chaos. If our expectations of what leadership is and can be are dominated by these negative cultural images, it is no wonder that we are ambivalent in our efforts to deal with leadership in the community of faith. This ambivalence is often deepened by our confusion over the place of power in a religious group.

IMAGES OF POWER IN THE RELIGIOUS GROUP

As Catholics these cultural images of power are not the only ones to influence our expectations about leadership. Leadership in the community of faith involves not only social power but religious authority as well. As the work of sociologist Richard Schoenherr shows, there are images and expectations of religious power that influence the ways that authority functions in religious groups. Schoenherr is the Director of the Comparative Religious Organizations Studies Project at the University of Wisconsin in Madison, through which he has been involved in an ongoing analysis of the organizational structures and decision-making processes of the Catholic Church in this country. In his paper, "Power and Authority in Organized Religion," Schoenherr notes that much of what social scientists have learned about the patterns of power in secular organizations has been found to apply in religious organizations as well. But there remain important differences between religious organizations and other social systems. One of the most substantial differences, as Schoenherr demonstrates, is in the orientation to organizational power.

Schoenherr identifies two necessary, and necessarily opposing, movements of power in religious organizations. By nature religious groups foster patterns of social power that tend toward ever greater centralization, even as they foster movements of social power that necessarily tend toward radical decentralization. This is not to recommend one of these tendencies as "right" and the other as "wrong." It is not to suggest that one is "better" or "more religious" than the other. It is rather to note that each is essential to the vitality of the ongoing religious group and that the accompanying tension between these two tendencies is a normal experience in the life of the religious organization.

Religious groups grow out of an experience of transcendence. Across differing religious traditions this originating experience is almost universally spoken of as a personal encounter with power—power unlike any experienced elsewhere (therefore its transcendent quality), but power nonetheless. Religious groups both generate and are generated by this transforming experience. For most believers it is within a religious community that their original faith encounter takes place. And it is those who have experienced this transcendent power who act together in faith communities. If these religious groups are to function well and to continue over time, the normal requirements of organizational structure must be met. Important among these are the patterns of social power, leadership, authority, and control. But in principle, even if not always in practice, these patterns of social power can never claim ultimate legitimacy. The basic religious action of conversion is a movement of transformation through which believers come into a new relationship with God. The structures and formulations that organize the social life of religious groups are important to this movement of personal conversion, but they are neither its guarantee nor its goal. The religious organization does not have exclusive access to transforming power; by its own experience and proclamation the group knows God cannot be limited in this way.

Religious groups live in the paradox of these convictions: that the power of God genuinely abides within the group and that the group is not itself identical with the power of God; that the religious organization exists as a conduit of God's power and that God continues to act beyond this institution as well. The social structure of religious groups, then, necessarily reflects the tensions of this paradox.

Religious groups experience the demands of these two opposing movements of power. These tendencies, both essential to the ongoing community of faith, reflect the dual function of a religious organization. The goal of any religious group is twofold: first, to preserve the truth of the group's original transforming encounter with God, and second, to continue to invite persons into such a transforming personal encounter with God. To succeed, then, the religious group must encourage among its members ways of acting that achieve each of these goals. Over time these characteristic "ways of acting" within the group, these patterns of social behavior, become established organizational structures. But the structures that develop to serve the two equally essential goals, as Schoenherr shows, have sufficiently different effects that they will often be experienced as working against one another.

The centralizing tendency in religious groups is in the service of the first goal: to preserve the connection with the original encounter with God that stands "at the beginning" of the group's religious history and at the core of its ongoing religious identity. The effort to safeguard the memory of this originating experience of God exerts centripetal force, moving the group toward patterns of centralized social power. If it is to continue to be able to "tell the truth" about its own initial experience of God, the religious group must develop structures to help guarantee that its present is connected with its past. Often this concern for fidelity to origins is served by centralized patterns of authority, through which the social power of the group speaks univocally. Such patterns may have the complexity of the Catholic Church, where the pope stands as the ultimate authority in a bureaucracy of international scope. In a small religious commune the pattern of centralization may take the shape of an insistence on unanimity in consensus decision-making. But the movement is the same, the development of centralized patterns of social power in the group in order to safeguard the originating connection with transcendent power.

This tendency toward centralization is not the only movement of power in religious groups. There is an equally necessary and, if the group is vital, equally strong movement of decentralization. It is a movement through which the power of the group, God's power in the group, escapes the confines of its pattern of social organization. This second movement of power serves the other basic goal of the religious group, its effort to invite and support believers in an ongoing interior relationship of faith. The religious organization exists to proclaim that such a relationship is possible, to foster this relationship in those who have experienced personal transformation, and to invite into this encounter those as yet untouched. In the religious group's understanding of itself, it knows this interior life of faith to take precedence over other organizational goals and interests. The goal of the religious group's activity, as Thomas Franklin O'Meara notes in *Theology of Ministry*, "is not ultimately membership or orthodoxy (although these are important, often crucial) but individual relationship with God, the process of becoming that which God's creative love intends in my birth, that is, radical salvation."[1]

This conviction grounds the centrifugal force of decentralization in religious organizations. Fostering the relationship of faith has priority over other institutional commitments and organizational goals. Here then is the essential decentralizing tendency in any religious organizaton. To achieve its purposes, the organization must support its members in their relationship with transcendent power and must nurture this relationship along its own unique path. In doing so, the organization strengthens the ability of local communities and individuals to stand apart. It confirms that these smaller groups may have the power and even the responsibility to stand "up to" and even "over against" the established social power within the organization.

In the religious group, then, the power that is at the foundation of things has at least two means of expression. The power of God can manifest itself both in conscience, personal and communal, and in centralized structures. The expectation in religious groups is that these two manifestations will be in concert; each will clarify and reinforce the other. And not a little energy is spent attempting to insure that God's will as manifest in centralized authority and God's will as manifest in conscience will be the same, or at least congruent. But at the core of the world view that grounds the religious group is a conviction of the sacredness of the personal relationship of faith. Ultimately this conviction relativizes all the structures of centralized social power within the group.

The tension, then, between God's power manifest in the conscience of believers and God's power manifest through the centralized processes of group authority is inevitable in religious organizations. Later in this volume, David Power discusses this tension in terms of the dialectic between "the free exercise of the gifts of the Spirit" and "the canonization of power for the common good." The challenge for the religious group is not to resolve this tension in the exclusive choice of one or the other, since *both* are religious power, manifestations of the power of God. This struggle cannot be "resolved" in this sense, or at least not without significant loss to the religious group. It is a continuing and necessary structural tension in any vital religious organization. What is required instead is that the religious group, as distinguished from other forms of social organization, develop patterns that acknowledge both forms of religious power and that incorporate and even celebrate the paradox of their more apparent contradiction.

One way of charting the history of a religious group is in terms of these two experiences of religious power. At different times in its history, the group's structure is likely to express different emphases in this dialectic of centralization and decentralization. In Roman Catholic experience the structural process of centralization reached its apogee at the Council of Trent, in part in response to the decentralization reinforced in the Reformation. This necessary, but necessarily partial, image of religious power continued to dominate Church life over the subsequent four centuries. Many of the reforms of the Second Vatican Council may be understood as attempts to reinstate the structures that respect the pluriformity of God's power among us and thus to reestablish the necessary tension between the centralization and decentralization of religious power.

This somewhat neutral statement may help us understand what is going on, but it does not do justice to the turmoil that has been experienced. A dramatic structural shift is involved as the international bureaucracy of Roman Catholicism attempts to reestablish organizational patterns that respect the religious power of believers and of the local Church. We are not yet very good at this, as the controversy over the role of national conferences of bishops shows. Even as we get better at it, what we will be guaranteeing by our new structures is not organizational peace but continuing organizational tension. This tension, as we have seen, is normal and even necessary for the religious vitality of the Church, but it is tension nonetheless. It is against such a background of complex expectations and conflicted history that we are attempting today to discern the forms of leadership that are emerging among us.

II. The Social Processes Involved in Leadership

Leadership refers to the exercise of initiative and influence in the achievement of a group's goals. Early attempts by social scientists to understand leadership most often focused on the person of the leader. The assumption was that leadership is a personality characteristic or trait, an ability that some of us have and others do not. Leadership was thus understood as a relatively stable quality that a person possesses either innately (those of us who are "born leaders") or by training.

Understood as a trait, leadership was presumed to be a somewhat consistent quality, expected to be exercised in the same way in whatever setting the leader found himself (the pronoun is appropriate here, since this understanding of leadership usually included the judgment that it was a properly "masculine" quality). In research the goal of this approach was to isolate certain personality traits that would identify those who could function as leaders in groups. The result would be a world divided into leaders and followers, with people falling into one category or the other depending on the presence or absence of this clearly definable personality trait. The assumption was that leadership is a univocal quality, such that a person who has it will be able to lead in almost all situations, and a person without it will be a follower most of the time.

This approach was abandoned in the social sciences after several decades of research failed to identify any such univocal trait. When real groups were studied, leaders could be identified and their traits could be discerned and described. The trouble was that this research turned up a remarkable array of characteristics among these actual leaders. From situation to situation, the personality characteristics of those persons who functioned effectively as leaders were much too diverse for leadership to be a single trait. Studies in different settings even came up with contradictory findings of what it takes to be a leader.

There is an awareness in the social sciences today that in approaching leadership as primarily an individual attribute we have been looking at the wrong thing. In focusing on individual behavior, we have narrowed our attention too quickly. Our preoccupation with the behavior of one of the individuals in the group, the person designated as the leader, has distracted us from what is going on in the group as a whole. Leadership is not just what one person in the group has; it is something that people in a group do together.

Within the social sciences, then, we can note a shift from seeing leadership as an attribute—something that a person has—to understanding it as a process—something that goes on among a group of people. This reinterpretation of leadership is part of a larger interest in the group understood as a whole, as a social system whose reality encompasses more than just the sum of its members taken individually.

THE GROUP AS A SOCIAL SYSTEM

For most of us, it is not easy to think of the group as a reality. Our immediate awareness is that it is individuals who are "real." "The group" is an abstraction, a collective term that gives us a shorthand way of talking about several people. But it is the individuals who are really "there." The group, then, is Mary plus Mark plus Jane plus John . . . , the sum of the members. However, the systematic study of groups over the past several decades has led analysts increasingly to the realization that groups are more than the sum of the persons who make them up. A group is a network of relationships. It is these relationships, the interconnections that develop between and among members, that constitute the group as an entity.

In his work at the Laboratory for the Study of Small Groups, at the University of Wisconsin, our colleague Gordon Myers uses the example of a microscope to help clarify the reality of the group as a whole. When we use a microscope to study an organism, we know that we will see different levels of activity at different settings of magnification. Sometimes we want to examine the activity of a single cell, but often we will be more interested in how the organism functions as a whole. No one setting on the microscope gives a view that is more "real" than another. It is rather the symptom or activity that we are trying to understand that helps us decide what level of magnification to choose. But the focus we set will determine what we see.

The same principle can be applied to the study of groups. Studying the members one at a time can tell us something about a group and its functioning, but not everything, and sometimes not what we most want to know. Some of the most significant information about groups remains invisible to us, if we focus on individuals and on the way that one member behaves toward another. Thus we come to see that groups are more than the neutral setting in which individuals deal with one another. The group is an entity. It has a life and function of its own, not apart from the members but with dimensions that go beyond the members taken as individuals or even as a collection of individuals. There is much about the life and functioning of a group that we will not be able to understand if we look just through the lens of personal behavior. It is not that the focus on individuals results in incorrect information, simply that it results in partial information. It does not tell us all there is to know about this group, sometimes it does not tell us what is most important. What we tend to miss as we focus on individuals is the pattern of interaction that constitutes the group as a whole. To explore this pattern of interaction, this active network of interconnectedness, is to examine the group as a social system.

Leadership is a characteristic of the social system more than of any single person within the group. It is in the group as a whole that leadership happens. When we see a group functioning well, in ways that are satisfying for the members and effective in accomplishing their purposes, we say the group has leadership. In ordinary speech we often assign leadership to those persons in the group whom we sense to be somehow responsible for things going well. But, in a social systems understanding, leadership "belongs" properly to the group as a whole. Leadership is first a quality of the group's activity and only secondarily a characteristic of individuals in the group.

LEADERSHIP AS A GROUP PROCESS

Leadership is a social transaction: it is what goes on in a group to enable members to mobilize their power in order to achieve their common goals. Over time every group of people develops a more or less characteristic way of bringing its resources to bear to get what it wants or needs. Roommates decide how household chores will be divided. A ministry team determines who among them is best at running the weekly staff meeting and who is best at leading the group in a day of prayer. A diocesan pastoral council works out an organizational chart to clarify the relationship between diocesan responsibility and parish responsibility. Sometimes this arrangement of "who does what to help us get what we need" is worked out informally: "people here just do what they are good at and somehow all the work gets done." But more often there are formal patterns that develop as well. In roles and offices, in contracts and bylaws, we set out more explicitly the responsibilities we have to one another and to our common tasks. This, then, is the leadership process, the pattern of formal and informal arrangements through which a group acts effectively.

LEADERSHIP AS A PROCESS OF POWER

The leadership process, as the somewhat enduring pattern of initiative and influence among us, is an expression of power. A group's patterns of leadership reflect how it understands power to be distributed within the group. What kinds of strength are important to us? Who among us is strong in this way? Where does this strength come from? How is it to be used? The processes of leadership in any group are, in part, its answers to these questions. The practice of leadership describes how these resources of power are actually put to work. Leadership patterns reflect a group's awareness of differences in power and what these differences mean. We do not all possess equally the kinds of "strength" that are important in this group, whether that be physical prowess, skill, money, or holiness. This issue of unequal strength is perhaps the most challenging aspect of social power. What are the relationships that develop among us because of these differences? How do we respond to the inequalities in strength that are inevitably a part of our life together?

Attitudes toward power and understandings of its role are at the core of a group's leadership processes. In ordinary awareness power always involves an experience of strength. But to say power is to say more than strength alone. Power is strength *in relation to* something. Definitions of power in the social sciences characteristically acknowledge this relational aspect. Power is discussed as a social transaction, but the transaction tends to be described as a one-way process. The analogue is physical strength: we say someone is powerful physically when the person is strong *in relation to* physical objects, able to lift a heavy weight or to move a large obstacle. Similarly, this understanding goes, a person who is socially powerful is strong *in relation to* other people, able to influence their judgments or control their actions.

Power is thus defined as the ability to influence others or, correlatively, to resist being influenced by them. The underlying model of the power transaction here is "A affects B"; the relation is unilateral. In this understanding power resides in the agent stance. To *be influenced* is thus to lack power. In such an interpretation receptivity easily becomes understood as passivity and as weakness. In many sociological discussions of leadership, these dichotomies of active/passive and strong/weak are the dominant categories through which social relations are understood.

Currently this unilateral interpretation of the social process of power is being challenged both from within and from without the social sciences. In *Powers of the Weak* Elizabeth Janeway draws together several strands of this dissent. She cites the growing body of research findings that show patterns of *reciprocal* interaction and *mutual* dependence to characterize transactions of power. To be powerful is to participate in a relationship of strength. But the modes of participation are not simply the polar opposites of active/passive or strong/weak. Social power is not unilateral but reciprocal. To be powerful is to be able to participate in the flow of this reciprocal relationship. Janeway goes on to explore the "powers of the weak," the concrete ways in which subordinate parties participate in the dynamic of social power.

From a perspective outside the social sciences, theologian Bernard Loomer goes even further in the recognition of the role of recipient power. In his paper "Two Kinds of Power," strongly influenced by process thought, Loomer stresses the bilateral quality of power. Any understanding of power which is limited to the unilateral image is necessarily deficient, since it fails to recognize the most central element of social transaction, its relational aspect. For Loomer relational power is manifest in a readiness to take account of the feelings and values of another, and thus to include the other within one's world of meaning and concern. "From this perspective," Loomer suggests, "power is neither the capacity to produce nor undergo an effect. Power is the capacity to sustain a mutually internal relationship."[2]

Unilateral images of power stand behind the structures of most organizations today, whether corporations, service agencies, educational institutions, or religious groups. In these organizational settings leadership behavior is usually understood as unilateral power exercised within a hierarchical structure. To the degree that unilateral images are dominant, leadership is understood predominantly in terms of agent behavior and control.

As the relational dynamics of social power are better understood, the limits of these current organizational structures of leadership are better appreciated. The critique of unilateral leadership is well underway in the management sciences. In *Collaboration in Organizations*, for example, management analyst William Kraus urges a review of the central values of competition and status that underlie hierarchical models of organizational life. As Paul Hersey and Kenneth Blanchard document in *Management of Organizational Behavior*, relational images are gradually beginning to influence the functions of power and leadership in American corporate structure. It is an irony that unilateral power images continue to shape leadership roles in so much of organized church life, while relational images of power are at the core of its religious belief. The chapters by John Shea, David Power, and James Whitehead in this volume trace several of these core images of power in the Christian tradition.

III. The Dynamics of Leadership in the Group Setting

Leadership, as we have seen, is a process of group interaction that is related to power. At different points in a group's life, the shape of its leadership will be different. As social processes and priorities within the group change, so its patterns of initiative and influence take on different form. We will examine first, the shifting priorities experienced over the life of a group and second, the leadership demands that are related to these different phases of the group's experience.

PRIORITY ISSUES IN THE LIFE OF THE GROUP

Life in a group is not static. There is movement and activity and change. Over the last several decades social psychologists have been intrigued by the possibility that there is an overarching pattern in this movement, a sequence of change to be found in the experience of group life. Research interest has been high; in *The Life Cycle of Groups*, for example, Roy Lacoursiere reviews over eighty studies of small group phase development. These investigations reveal a pattern of shifting priorities in the ways members act toward one another and toward their tasks. This pattern, found repeated in groups of many different kinds, is often described in terms of the stages in the life cycle of a group.

There is some controversy over the adequacy of the notion of "stages" to explain this regular pattern. To some the term seems to claim too much, suggesting an inner determinism and inevitability that go beyond what we really know. These analysts prefer to speak of phases of group experience or shifts in the focus of group interaction. But, even with this caution concerning terminology, most serious students of group life agree that there is an expectable sequence in the pattern of life together in groups.

Our preference here is to discuss this movement in terms of a series of issues that demand attention over the course of a group's life. All the issues are relevant to the group throughout its life, but all are not equally "live issues" all the time. The best image, perhaps, is one of shifting priorities: at different moments in our life together as a group, different questions come to "center stage" and demand more of our time and energy. There is some sequence involved; questions of "who belongs," for example, are likely to precede questions of "what can we accomplish together." But the sequence is expectable, not inevitable. In any particular case factors within the group or forces outside may influence the timing and intensity and sequence of these issues.

These changing patterns of priority can be understood as movements of the group as a whole, as when we say "the group is excited about its future" or "the group is looking outside itself for an answer" or "the group is feeling strong." The patterns can also be examined in terms of the demands and expectations that arise. At different times in the group's development, members have different expectations of themselves and one another; they make different demands of the designated leader and others who are judged to have power in the group. As we have seen, leadership processes are closely related to a group's sense of where power exists and how it can be exercised among the members. These questions of social power are renegotiated in each phase of group development. Thus a central part of our exploration of leadership is an examination of how the processes of social power function at different points in the group's life.

Several formulations of the pattern of group development are available, ranging from the classic distinction between autonomy issues and intimacy issues made by Warren Bennis and H. A. Sheppard in the 1950's to the more sophisticated matrix model currently being tested by Robert Boyd. Whatever their complexity, these statements tend to concur in the general shape and sequence of the issues involved. While the model sketched here is somewhat condensed, it represents a current consensus. In this discussion of group development and the analysis of leadership that follows, I am indebted to the work of Gordon Myers at the Laboratory for the Study of Small Groups.

Four central issues of group interaction are inclusion, power, intimacy, and effectiveness.

Inclusion

At issue here is who belongs. For the individual this can be the question of whether I am really a member of this group and how I go about deciding this. Do I really belong here? To answer the question, I may look inside to determine how I feel about the group and my place in it. I may look outside myself for signs that this is a group I want and for assurances that I am really wanted here. For the group as a whole, this issue may take the shape of the question of identity. Who are we as a group? What brought us together originally? What holds us together now?

These questions of identity are likely to absorb the attention of any group that is coming together for the first time. People attempt to size up each other, both to learn about these other people and to determine whether I want to—or am equal to—being with them in a group. The inclusion question is likely to arise again at any point of crisis or significant change for the group, in membership, in leadership, in purpose. As this question comes into focus again in a group already formed, it is often experienced as a loss of a sense of cohesion among us, as members pull back to explore the issues of who belongs now, do I still belong, who are we now as a group.

Power

A second issue in the ongoing process of coming together as a group is that of power. What kind of strength is important in this group? Who among us has that kind of power? How strong am I in this group? Where do I stand in regard to the power structure here? Will I be able to join it, to influence it? For some individuals these questions may influence the early experience of inclusion: I belong where I have some sense of personal power. For power issues to become a group focus, however, there must be a number of people with at least an initial sense of inclusion or belonging. Only then will questions of power be engaged. Thus the movement into the power struggle marks a new level of group maturity. In some settings the power issues are worked in discussions of goals and expectations and in negotiations around rules and roles. Through these efforts members come to a better sense of the structure of influence and initiative that exists among them and "where I fit" within it. In other groups this power struggle lives up to its name, taking the form of conflict and other disruptive behavior. Members may attack one another or blame the leader or turn against the group as a whole. The goal is the same, to establish and test the pattern of power among us and to find one's place in it.

When power issues come to the fore, the group is likely to experience a good deal of strain. Sometimes there is open hostility that must be faced. Even without this, there is often anxiety, misunderstanding, and blame. These negative emotions are seldom pleasant, but they are often part of a group's development. Indeed, the emergence of power issues often indicates that members are engaged. The experience of conflict may well signal that a level of group commitment and effectiveness is possible now that was not possible before. For conflict to lead the group to this new level of maturity, it will need to be handled well, and this is not always easy. But it is important that we be able to see the issues of power and conflict in the group for what they are, not simply and automatically a sign that the group is in trouble but rather an indication that a new phase of group life is being approached.

Intimacy

In most group settings it is only after the early power issues are faced that the questions of closeness can arise. What are the ways in which we stand "up close" in this group? How close do we want to be to one another here? What can the members of this group expect from one another? What do we have to give and receive from each other? For the individual the question may be: Can this group meet my needs? Which of my needs is it legitimate to bring to this group? Am I willing to respond to the needs of others here? For the group as a whole the challenge now is to work out the most satisfying ways of interrelating.

There is a wide range of possible responses to the questions of closeness in a group. Some groups develop strong networks of emotional support among members. Others tend toward "cooler" patterns, in which emotional sharing is at a minimum. Neither trend is, of itself, better or "more mature." The optimal level of emotional intimacy will depend on many factors of group composition, norms, and goals. Each group, however, has to negotiate the question of emotional closeness as it establishes the patterns of relating that are appropriate among its members. The process of working out these patterns is ongoing, but there are times in a group's life when these issues of "who are we for one another" come into special focus. Here, as in the power issues, the emergence of the questions can be threatening. For some a focus on what is going on among us is a sign that the group has gotten off track: "We are here to do a job; it is a waste of time to be talking so much about ourselves and each other." For others it is embarrassing to admit wanting or needing anything from others. Sensitivity is required as issues of closeness are faced. But here again, as in conflict, the emergence of these questions is most often an indication that a new stage of maturity is now possible.

Effectiveness

These are the questions that focus on the group's goals or external tasks. What can we achieve together? How do we marshal our diverse talents and energy for the work that confronts us? For the individual the questions are: What can I accomplish with this group that goes beyond what I can do on my own? How will the group make use of my contribution? The challenge for the group is to develop ways to bring its resources to bear on its common tasks. Patterns of decision-making, motivation, and coordination become key. At this point in its development, the group's priority is its work. The group's activity is concentrated on generating and using its resources of talent, money, skills, and personnel. At the same time group participation is high, with members encouraging and assisting one another in the work. As a result the general level of group satisfaction tends to be high as well. The tension between "people issues" and "task issues" fades, as members experience both their work and their relationships thriving.

This period of high group effectiveness is not without distress, since the demands of the task can be considerable and group resources may well be strained, but morale is high. There is the sense that one is getting back from the group at least as much as one is required to give. The costs of group membership seem amply compensated by the rewards that come along with it.

This phase in group life does not last indefinitely. Changing external circumstances, internal group fatigue, or any number of other factors can interrupt the process of group effectiveness. This interruption is frequently sensed in a shift in the group's internal priorities, as one of the other, developmentally "earlier" questions moves to center stage. It is inclusion or power or intimacy that is now at stake. Sometimes this shift is truly a regressive move, taking the group back to a set of earlier, probably unresolved, issues within its life. More often, though, the reemergence of these issues is not regression but, again, an invitation to move forward. The "old" question is asked anew, as a way of generating a new response in the group, one more consonant with the new level of maturity now available to it.

LEADERSHIP IN GROUP DEVELOPMENT

The leadership patterns in a group change as these different issues emerge. Each shift in initiative and influence involves a different awareness of the power of the group itself. This in turn results in differing needs experienced by the group as a system and in different demands made on the group's designated leader or leaders. Some of these demands are sound, in that, if met well, they move the group to a higher level of functioning. Other demands made of leaders are more problematic, distracting a group from moving on in its task. The response of the designated leader to these shifting demands is critical in determining whether a group stagnates or moves forward in its communal life.

Inclusion

At this early point in a group's coming together, as well as at other times when belonging is an issue, the group's sense of its own power is minimal. There is, as yet, no "us" to count on. The tendency is to look outside for answers and assurances. Individuals will look to the person who has been designated as leader, expecting here to find personal recognition and approval. This formal leader will be expected as well to provide answers to the question "who are we as a group." Since answers are sensed to be within the power of the leader, confusion and ambiguity over the group's goals—very normal at this stage—will be felt to be the leader's "fault." If there is as yet no formal leader, the group is likely to cast in this role one of its members whom it senses to be "powerful" by some outside criteria. Thus a man is often looked to before a woman, a priest or religious rather than a layperson, a professional over a workingclass person, a person with credentials over a volunteer. If the designated leader will not or cannot help the group deal with these early issues of inclusion and identity, anger and frustration will result. When personal investment in the group is high enough, this frustration can lead the members to turn away from the designated leader and look elsewhere for the power they need. Often, though, the group simply disbands.

At this stage in a group's life, there is pressure on the designated leader to function as a dominant, even parental, figure. The dominant leader can serve the group's development here by providing structures that help group members to get to know one another and to clarify their expectations, and by modeling the kind of behavior that will help the group to be effective. But early dominant leadership can also be a trap if it establishes a long-term expectation that it is the designated leader who is responsible for meeting the needs of the group. In this case both leader and group fall victim to the illusion that the group's power resides in the designated leader. Over time the demands made on the leader increase dramatically, as does the resentment and frustration within the group. The leader can be overwhelmed with the continuing needs of group members: for answers, for assurance, for the benefits of the leader's power. The leader can feel consumed by these demands, then gradually resentful of the dependence of the group, and finally alienated from these "needy" followers who seem only to take and to give nothing (but deference) in return.

The group members, for their part, experience growing resentment and bitterness as well. The dominance that served to allay anxiety in the group's early stages now seems to foster frustration. Once the pattern is established that only the leader has the power to meet our needs, then our resentment of the leader grows even as our sense of personal power declines. The bond with the leader that we experienced earlier as gratitude we now feel only as a reminder and reinforcement of our need. The style of leadership we discussed earlier as paternalism is the potential outcome if the designated leader continues too long to dominate the life of a group.

Power

When the power issues come to the fore, it is most often designated leadership that falls under attack. Power questions arise in a group in the tension around dependence. Very often this friction first takes the form of an attack on the established patterns of leadership. A member or a subgroup takes a stand that challenges the way that things are going. If the designated leader responds to this as a personal challenge, the battle is joined. Other members feel pressured to take sides; sometimes they unite in a shaky coalition "against" the leader. What is going on is a process of power redistribution. As the "we" of the group takes shape, members begin to sense the discrepancy that has existed between the leader and "the rest of us." This power discrepancy, which was acceptable and even desirable to group members early on, now seems an insult. The effort is to get the leader into the group as "just one of us," or to drive the leader out.

As we saw earlier, the emergence of the power struggle is often a sign of growth in the group. Members become aware of their earlier dependence on the designated leader and sense that to continue this pattern would not be good. They may respond with counterdependence. This attempt to dismantle the no longer useful pattern of power may take the shape of an enforced equality, the refusal to permit any power differences to be acknowledged. "We are all equals here, no one is more in charge than anyone else." Or its form may be one of substitution: "our choice" is put into the designated leader's slot, leaving the patterns of unequal dependence intact. With the dynamics of leadership left unchanged, it is not long before "our choice" becomes "the enemy" and another coup is called for.

The way out of this vicious cycle is to focus the effort of change not on the leader but on the patterns of leadership. What needs to be reinterpreted is where power exists and how power functions among us. The designated leader is only part of this larger design of social power in the group. It is only as a larger redesign is undertaken that it is safe to have the designated leader among us again, safe for both the group and the person in that role.

The designated leader can be more than a victim of this process. The way that the leader responds to the initial power challenge has significant influence on the group's move beyond dependence. The designated leader is usually in a position of some considerable power when the first questioning of leadership occurs. If the leader uses that power against the group member who questions, the rest of the group learns that new patterns of power will not be easily won. The message is given that the stakes are high in the process of change. If, however, the designated leader does not respond to this question as though it were a personal attack, a different tale is told. The message here is that power in the group need not be interpreted as a personal possession and jealously guarded against any loss. Rather, it is a resource of the group that can be examined, accounted for, and even redistributed among the group members.

Intimacy

When it is questions of closeness that are of greatest significance to a group, the role of the designated leader becomes crucial in another way. It is not unusual for the intimacy issue to become focused on the person of the leader. The leader is seen as the one who should satisfy the interpersonal needs of the members of the group. Each member seeks a "special" relationship with the leader. This relationship is seen as more satisfying than any that members might develop among themselves. It is emotional closeness with the leader that is valued. The development of bonds among group members is downplayed or even discouraged. In some groups this focus on the leader is a part of explicit policy. The goal is an allegiance to the leader unclouded by competing emotional commitments. But in many groups these emotional dynamics of exclusivity are not sought after; they are not even understood. Furthermore, they function to complicate the experience of group cohesion and effectiveness.

A group matures in the area of intimacy to the degree that it develops satisfying ways for members to give and receive from one another and not just from the leader. The behavior of the designated leader is important here. If the leader needs to be the exclusive focus of emotion in the group, this movement of group maturity will be held back. The group's energy will be consumed instead in the volatile issues of love and hate, favoritism and jealousy, allegiance and disloyalty. To assist a group at this stage in its development, the designated leader needs to model the kind of closeness that is desirable among group members and to encourage the development of these bonds. There is danger to the group's development if relationships with the leader become too personalized, if one feels identity with the group only through an intense relationship with the leader. In most settings it helps for the leader to be personable, but not to become the sole focus of affection and emotion.

Again, it is important to remember that significant emotional closeness is not a useful expectation in many groups, perhaps even in most. Deep friendship and devoted personal love are special relationships and necessarily rare. To mature as a group does not require the establishment of these bonds of deep emotional mutuality. But it does mean to establish *some* patterns of mutuality, some generally acceptable sense of what group members want to give and receive from one another at the personal level, however modest these expectations may be.

Beyond modeling this kind of mutuality, the leader can also facilitate the development of ties among group members. The designated leader is often in a position to help set in place structures that encourage interaction among members. Included here are procedures that encourage cooperative work as well as opportunities for more informal social sharing. Alert to the emotional dimensions of the group's life, the designated leader can help the group deal more explicitly with its own issues of closeness by helping group members clarify their expectations and establish patterns of mutual support that draw on the broad resources of the group as a whole.

Effectiveness

As its attention shifts to the larger goal or task that brought members together, the group experiences different concerns. Its chief priorities now are clarity about its task and the effective use of its resources to meet this goal. At this stage in a maturing group, the sense of personal power and group resourcefulness is high. The most effective focus of the leader's impact and influence at this point is the group itself. The leader's role now is not to do the task but to help the group insure that the task is done. To work effectively toward the group task, members need to sharpen their understanding of the common goal, to be motivated to contribute their best resources, and to coordinate their talents and skills in ways that achieve optimum effect. Even here, in groups that are working well, many aspects of these control and coordination functions are shared among group members rather than left as the sole responsibility of the leader. Patterns of shared information and decision-making are likely to develop, along with collaborative action and accountability among members. The designated leader is expected to keep this larger vision before the group and to help keep the group's activities on track, but neither the vision nor the task "belongs" to the leader. The designated leader functions at this phase as custodian of the group's vision and facilitator of its task.

One temptation of groups at this stage is for the leader to be seen as the one who is really in charge. If the issues of group identity, power, and intimacy have not been sufficiently resolved, members are not likely to face their external task with much sense of the group's competence and confidence. The designated leader then remains the only figure in the group who is seen to know what should be done and how to go about it. Since the task is "really" the leader's, the commitment of the other members is minimal. The designated leader in this kind of group can feel abandoned in the work. The leader can feel that it is easier to do the work directly and alone than to try to involve this passive and resistant group.

Another temptation of the group at this stage is, in its enthusiasm for the task, to give itself over to the rational aspects of its goal-directed activities. The demands of productivity are taken seriously, the goals of achievement are made clear, a healthy competition may even develop among members in their investment in the task. These goal-directed activities are assisted by the rational strategies of problem-solving and decision-making. Frequently, it is the designated leader who is responsible, not for solving the problems or making the decisions but for insuring that these cognitive strategies operate in the group to help it meet its tasks. These rational efforts can absorb the leader's attention as well as that of the other members, casting the designated leader as predominantly a task figure and leaving the group's interaction too exclusively focused on achievement. When this happens, other aspects of the group's life are likely to be overlooked.

The extrarational dynamics of shared life often suffer during periods of high productivity. But it is at the extrarational level that group commitment is most deeply nourished. For the group to remain vital, these elements of cohesion and commitment, of symbol and celebration, must be tended. These are the dynamics that nourish a sense of mutual concern and loyalty, keeping alive the shared dream that calls forth commitment over the long term, commitment to values and purposes that go beyond the task at hand.

The designated leader must be alert to this level of group interaction and aware of its importance. In some groups, especially religious groups, the designated leader is also seen as the person most directly responsible for nurturing the group at these deeper levels. Thus the religious group is likely to suffer if its designated leader does not or cannot respond to its extrarational needs. Here again, this does not mean that the designated leader should function as the exclusive resource to the group's needs for symbol and celebration, even in religious groups. In every group there are likely to be several persons with the strengths of imagination and talents of ritual and the arts that can enhance the extrarational life of the members. The designated leader's role may well be more that of calling out these talents and of insuring that the group takes time together both in ritual and play. Without these the group may well exhaust itself in the task and lose the savor of its deeper sense of purpose.

IV. The Role of the Designated Leader

In most groups, as we have seen, there is a designated leader, someone publicly acknowledged in a position that stands for the larger group. Often the designated leader "stands for" the common good; the leader is the person in the group charged with the responsibility to order its resources for the good of the whole. There are many dynamics that may place a person in that position: election or appointment, heredity or merit. In most settings designated leadership is, at least in part, managerial leadership. Many leadership titles point to the "ordering" responsibilities that go with the office—presiding (president), directing (director), coordinating (coordinator), governing (governor), shepherding (pastor). Sometimes another aspect of designated leadership is stressed in the title: the leader's priority over the other members. We see this in those titles of leadership that emphasize the status that goes with the job, titles such as superior, eminence, primate, mayor.

The designated leader is not always in a management role, but this is the usual pattern. The leader has some special or final say in regard to the group's activities and personnel and money. The designated leader is seldom *just* an orderer of resources, but this control function is the base of much of the influence that the leader has in the ongoing life of the group.

The ordering function of the designated leader need not be limited to material resources. In a group that is functioning well, the designated leader is likely to give more attention to nurturing a shared vision and motivating the members to use their talent to pursue these common goals. It is at this level of interaction that the common good is most effectively pursued.

The designated leader "stands for" the group externally as well. It is often this leader who represents the group in the larger public world: the leader is invited to represent the group at a city-wide celebration; the media contact the leader for a public statement or to learn where the group stands on an issue; in public behavior and in private life the leader is expected to "practice" what the group "preaches."

In a bureaucracy the designated leader is also the link between the group and the larger organizational system. This link can generate additional ambiguity in the leadership processes. Is the leader's first loyalty to the group or to the larger organization? The leader's allegiance to the group can be especially suspect when, as is the case in most bureaucratic structures, the larger system places the person in the position as designated leader. Both the leader and the group know that this position can be a stepping-stone in a larger process of bureaucratic advancement, if the leader's tenure goes well.

Much of the tension experienced today around the roles of bishop, pastor, and, to a lesser extent, religious superior flows from this ambiguous positioning. Does the designated leader represent the organization—bringing its agenda and resources to the group—or the group—bringing its needs and perspective back to the organization? In the understanding that prevailed among us before the Second Vatican Council, this tension was at a minimum. The good pastor could be expected to care for his parishioners, but he stood in their midst not as "one of them" but as a representative of the universal Church. He held his religious power and his jurisdiction in trust, accountable to those above him in the religious hierarchy. Today there is a greater expectation that the designated leader belongs to the group and represents its needs and interests. The leader is becoming accountable to the group as well as to the organization. His (and increasingly, her) duty is to represent the group to the larger organization as much as to uphold the interests of the organization in the context of the group. Here, as in the earlier discussion of Schoenherr's analysis of the contrast in orientations to power in the religious group, we touch on a necessary structural tension, one that is likely to increase rather than decrease over the coming decades in the American Church.

By this point in our discussion, it should be clear that the designated leader is only one of the factors contributing to group effectiveness. When this reality of group life is not understood, both the group and the leader are in trouble. When a group functions in such a way that it *expects* influence and intiative only from its designated leader, the burdens of leadership become immense. The leader is seen, often by self as well as by others, to be personally responsible for everything—the formulation of vision, the achievement of goals, the satisfaction of needs, the quality of group interaction. If the group accepts influence and initiative only from its designated leader, it stagnates. Some members leave. Those who stay, either by choice or coercion, gradually become less engaged and contribute less of themselves to the group's life. When it is only the designated leader who is powerful, the antagonisms of internal politics intensify. Much of the skill and energy of members will be spent not in the larger tasks of group effectiveness but in internecine power struggles.

THE SENSE OF PERSONAL POWER IN LEADERSHIP

To this point we have spoken of power primarily in its social face. Power has been discussed as a social transaction, as a group pattern of initiative and influence. There is also a personal face to power. Personal power has to do with how I experience myself as strong. Sometimes this awareness focuses on the substance of my strength: my talents, competence, influence, reputation, and the like. Sometimes the awareness of personal power includes a more complex realization of where my strength comes from and what it is for.

The work of psychologist David McClelland contributes to an understanding of personal power in the experience of the designated leader. In *Power: The Inner Experience* McClelland investigates the relationship between attitudes about personal power and the level of psychological maturity. "Need for power," as McClelland and his colleagues specify it, is a concern about influencing others. Along with the need for achievement (concern about doing things well) and need for affiliation (concern about making friends), the need for power describes an important part of the adult experience of maturity. In his research McClelland found that this need for power takes different shapes. In some it finds expression in the accumulation of possessions; in others, in pride of self-sufficiency.

Some adults express power concerns through direct aggressive behavior. Others work more indirectly, through strategies of influence, suggestion, and inspiration.

A mistaken assumption of common sense is that all leadership positions require high power motivation. McClelland's study of effective leaders in large organizations reveals a more nuanced picture. Designated leaders who were successful in their roles ranked moderately high in an awareness of their own power and in concern for issues of influence and control, but they were seldom the persons with the highest power scores. These successful leaders displayed a more balanced motivation profile. Their concern for personal influence was balanced by equally high motives of achievement, the desire to do a good job, and affiliation, the desire to be in positive relationship with their coworkers. McClelland concludes that in many organizations the leader's task is more integrative than directive. A designated leader must show initiative and influence, but an organizational leader too concerned with these aspects of the role is likely to spend too little time integrating conflicting viewpoints.

Designated leadership involves two faces of personal power, dominance and organization. The personally dominant leader can be effective in some settings—a teenage gang, a military unit in battle—where the ruling image of power is physical strength in one-to-one conflict. But a leader who feels powerful only in face-to-face dominance moves quickly into a stance of personal authoritarianism: "my way is the right way." In the organizational setting the dominant leader's enthusiasm for certain goals can become an insistence that these goals are the right ones, the only ones, whatever the others in the group may think. Such a dictatorial stance seldom serves an organization well.

In most groups the designated leader is not to replace the ideas and talents of the members but to enlist these resources for the group task. This requires, in McClelland's terms, a more "socialized" type of leadership, a sense of personal power that can find expression in motivating, facilitating, and coordinating the activities of others.

The successful leaders whom McClelland studied were able to show both these faces of personal power, the organizational skills necessary to respect and coordinate the diverse energies of the group and the personal assertiveness necessary to inspire the allegiance and commitment of group members. Most of these leaders reported tension as they worked out the balance between expressing personal assertion and exercising a more "group-centered" style of leadership. Importantly, though, they were able to *feel powerful* in both these stances in the group. Therefore it was possible for them to display both kinds of behavior. The tension was experienced in the judgment about which kind of personal power was appropriate at this time, not whether to be powerful or impotent in the group. The more ways in which the leader can feel powerful, can experience personal power, the broader the range of leadership behavior that person has available. Feeling powerful is, as we have seen above in McClelland's research, not the only factor that motivates effective leaders, but it is an important factor. The more ways in which the sense of personal power can be expressed, the broader the range of alternative behaviors that the leader can draw upon easily. This flexibility adds much to the effectiveness of the designated leader and, through the leader, to the effectiveness of the group as a whole.

In an important aside McClelland notes that in order to develop the range of this more mature capacity for leadership, many men had to overcome patterns of personal dominance they had learned earlier as part of a conventional model of adult male behavior. To mature as designated leaders, many women, however, needed to develop stronger patterns of personal dominance and social assertiveness, patterns that were absent from their earlier socialization. In *Women, Men, and the Psychology of Power*, social psychologist Hilary Lips broadens this discussion of the similarities and differences between many women and men in their experiences and expression of power.

V. Learnings for the Community of Faith

How does this information contribute to the Church's reflection on its experience of leadership in ministry today? What here is of value in the effort to develop more adequate structures of mutual service and mutual empowerment in the community of faith? We offer here, in summary statement, several convictions central to the understanding of leadership in the social sciences today that seem relevant to an understanding of the current experience of leadership in the Church.

Leadership refers to the patterns of initiative and influence that develop in a group. Leadership is thus more a characteristic of a social setting than it is an attribute of an individual. The person who is designated as leader, while significant, is only part of the patterns of social power that emerge in any group. An awareness of this larger context, within which personal leadership behavior is situated, leads to more realistic, and frequently more modest, expectations of the designated leader.

The leadership patterns in a group are related to the group's phase of development. Different patterns of initiative and influence prevail at different points in a group's life. Whatever the stage in a group's life, the attitudes and behavior of the designated leader are crucial to the effectiveness of these larger patterns of initiative and influence. The designated leader can encourage or impede the group's development and the emergence of more mature patterns of leadership in the group as a whole.

Religious groups are similar to other groups in many ways. Thus many of the insights of organizational development apply in these settings. But religious groups have a unique and paradoxical orientation toward power that influences the expectation and experience of leadership, designated and otherwise. Several structural tensions derive from this religious ambivalence toward power and can be expected to continue as part of the experience of leadership in the faith community. These include: tension between the patterns that safeguard God's power as manifest through the organized life of the religious institution and those that safeguard God's power as manifest through the local group and the personal experience of faith; tension between the designated leader's responsibility to the group and to the larger religious institution; tension over the proper exercise of power by the designated leader and by others in the group or the group as a whole; tension between personal assertion and coordination skills in the leader's personal style.

Personal holiness, group maturity, and skillful behavior will each contribute to the vitality of religious organizations, but none of these can be expected to resolve the structural tensions that surround the exercise of power in the community of faith. This tension is a visible face of the paradox of power in the religious group.

Footnotes

1. Thomas Franklin O'Meara, *Theology of Ministry* (New York: Paulist Pres, 1983) 32–33.

2. Bernard Loomer, "Two Kinds of Power," *Criterion: Journal of the University of Chicago Divinity School* 15 (Winter 1976) 23.

References

Boyd, Robert D., "A Matrix Model of the Small Group," *Small Group Behavior* 14 (November 1983) 405–418. An overview of his comprehensive model for understanding small groups in an open system perspective.

Hersey, Paul, and Blanchard, Kenneth H. *Management of Organizational Behavior.* 4th ed. San Diego: Learning Resources Corporation, 1983. A collection of essays representing the "state of the art" in the current discussion of situational leadership.

Janeway, Elizabeth. *Powers of the Weak.* New York: Knopf, 1981. An important discussion of power as a social relationship, stressing the role of subordinate parties (the "weak") in process of both stability and change.

Kraus, William A. *Collaboration in Organizations: Alternatives to Hierarchy.* New York: Human Sciences Press, 1980. A challenge from within the discipline of organization development, urging a review of the central values of competition and status that underlie much group structure.

Lacoursiere, Roy. *The Life Cycle of Groups. New York:* Human Sciences Press, 1980. A summary statement of recent research findings treating the issue of "stages" in group interaction.

Lips, Hilary M. *Women, Men, and the Psychology of Power.* Englewood Cliffs, N.J.: Prentice-Hall, 1981. An analysis, based on a wide range of recent research findings, of the place of power in relationships between women and men.

Loomer, Bernard. "Two Kinds of Power," *Criterion: Journal of the University of Chicago Divinity School* 15 (Winter 1976) 11–29. A discussion, from the perspective of process theology, of personal power as a capacity to sustain mutually transforming relationships.

McClelland, David C. *Power: The Inner Experience.* New York: Irvington, 1975. An innovative synthesis of research findings and theory concerning the relation between personal maturity and the exercise of power.

Myers, J. Gordon. *Grief Work as a Critical Condition for Small Group Phase Development.* 1986. Available through the Laboratory for the Study of Small Groups at the University of Wisconsin in Madison, Wisconsin. An exploration of the extrarational dynamics of small group interaction, stressing the role of grief in the processes of group maturing.

O'Meara, Thomas Franklin. *Theology of Ministry.* New York: Paulist Press, 1983. An important statement that includes both historical synthesis and constructive theological argument concerning the shape of ministry.

Schoenherr, Richard. "Power and Authority in Organized Religion." 1982. Paper available through the Comparative Religious Organizations Studies Publications at the University of Wisconsin in Madison, Wisconsin. A broad review of sociological theory concerning social power and religious organizations, which distinguishes two movements of power in necessary tension in religious groups.

Sennett, Richard. *Authority.* New York: Vintage, 1981. A provocative examination of the social images of authority that influence the exercise of leadership in contemporary Western culture.

3. STEWARDSHIP: THE DISCIPLE BECOMES A LEADER

James D. Whitehead

The Emergence of Leadership

As Christians we are invited into a community of disciples. We are, whatever our role or authority, followers of Jesus Christ. As disciples we participate in God's powerful presence. We are touched by this power in the belonging and reconciliations that our community provides us. We are also invited to touch this power in responsible contributions to the community.

A community of disciples is a place of mutual empowerment. Both gifted and wounded, we care for one another in a mood of mutuality. God's power finds tangible expression in the many strengths that appear in a community. These significant differences in ability and giftedness make us interdependent on each other, but do not afford any of us a privileged or superior status before God. The power we find in ourselves and the authority that our responsibilities call us to are rooted finally neither in us nor our role but in the Spirit who blows where the Spirit will.

This New Testament vision of a community of disciples does not yet account for the appearance of leadership. A disciple is a follower and an apprentice. A disciple is pledged to a master—for Christians, Jesus Christ. As disciples of Christ, we are well aware that the Lord is not physically present to us, guiding our community life with the sure instruction of a master. Instead, a Christian group, trusting the interior presence of Christ and the Spirit, must reflect, debate, and decide by which paths it will follow the Lord.

Who of us will guide and critique this communal effort of discipleship? Who will be our leaders?

The dualistic image of a Christian community as composed of disciples and the Lord presents special dangers in today's Church. A hierarchical inheritance has tended to make the distinction between lay Christians (disciples) and clergy (those who lead the community in Christ's name). The danger is, of course, that the clergy are compelled into the function of the Lord, while the laity are encouraged to an exclusive role as disciples and followers. As with any dichotomy, the growth of the disciples is jeopardized and the development of leaders is restricted to ancient and narrow routes. Leadership comes to be pictured as a power or possession of individuals, rather than being an aspect of the group's life.

There is much enthusiasm in the Church today for the encouragement of leaders *from within* communities of faith. Such an internal development of leaders may allow us to recover the communal nature of leadership. One way to trace such a hoped for growth is to observe how some disciples become leaders. We will be charting the movement from discipleship to stewardship.

While remaining followers, some of the disciples in a community are gifted for and called to leadership roles. The power of God, experienced variously in the plural gifts that comprise a Christian community, is "canonized" in offices of leadership. To ensure order within the community and to guarantee continuity with the community's past, some gifts of service must be structured into offices of leadership. How will Christians manage the tensions aroused by this uneven distribution of power within a community?

The role of leadership has been envisioned in most cultures in images of elevation: on a regal throne or a priestly high altar the leader is made "superior" to others in the community. Jesus urged his disciples to resist this pervasive model of leadership. In his own behavior he displayed a more mutual and lowly style of leading, submitting in the end only to the paradoxical elevation on a cross. Matthew's Gospel recalls Jesus insisting that his followers reject the images and vocabulary of leadership that suggest special status and superiority: "You, however, must not allow yourselves to be called rabbi, since you have only one Master, and you are all siblings" (Matt 23:8). Jesus continues:

> You must call no one on earth your father, since you have only one Father, and he is in heaven. Nor must you allow yourselves to be called teachers, for you have only one Teacher, the Christ. The

greatest among you must be your servant. Those who exalt themselves will be humbled, and those who humble themselves will be
exalted (Matt 23:9-12).

This powerful passage urges mutuality as the ideal of shared life
and service as the style of leadership. Honorific titles such as father
and master do not fit the mode of leadership that Christian disciples are to exercise.

From the outset the Christian tradition has stumbled in its efforts to live up to this extraordinary ideal of service in mutuality.
Often succumbing to the temptation to interpret leadership in terms
of privileged status and superiority (witnessed to in such titles as
"Your Eminence," and "princes of the Church"), we Christians have
frequently stranded the servant character of leadership in rhetoric.

As we attempt to recover the special Christian motif of servant
leadership, we need to admit that the image of a servant is an
anachronism today. The word recalls historical periods, more hap-
pily forgotten, of slavery and servitude. The "service" of leadership that Jesus insists on will not be that of a slave/master economy
but of a community of mutuality. A second characteristic of servanthood is its implication of powerlessness: the servant has few
rights and no power. Yet a leader is precisely one who must be powerful—to initiate, confront, heal, and endure. How shall we envision Christian leadership as at once an exercise of power and of
service?

An image in our religious heritage which may help us is that
of stewardship. A steward, both in the New Testament and elsewhere, is an authoritative servant. Stewardship is a leadership position reserved for experienced, capable persons. Yet, its power and
authority are exercised in the service of someone else, the lord, and
a larger cause, the household or community. This image of stewardship blends power with service and authority with dependency; in
so doing, it reminds us of the special dynamic of Christian leadership. An examination of stewardship in the New Testament and
its special invitations in contemporary Christian life may help us
recognize the future shape of Christian leadership.

The Steward in the New Testament

The image of the steward in the Christian Scriptures exhibits
a variety of intriguing nuances. Steward is an Anglo-Saxon trans-
lation of the Greek word *oikonomos*—the one who sees to the law
(*nomos*) of the household (*oikos*). The steward is the person who

oversees the domestic order, the rhythms, rules, and agreements by which a household or community thrives.

The word steward appears in the Gospels only in Luke's account, and then only at two points. The first appearance is the famous parable of the faithful steward in Luke 12. This story highlights three features of a steward. First, this person acts as a servant, rather than owner or master. Second, the main strength or virtue of a steward is a combination of wisdom and trustworthiness, an experienced dependability. Third, the context of this servant leadership is absence: the steward makes responsible decisions in the absence of the master or owner. Thus the steward's authority is borrowed, a "guest authority."

The second appearance of the steward in Luke is in the story of the unjust steward who, about to be fired, is astute enough to reduce what his master's debtors owe (Luke 16). Again the steward acts with a certain wisdom or shrewdness; the steward also acts on his own authority and in the absence of the master. Paul, in his first letter to the Corinthians, describes the same characteristics of the steward: such a person acts as a servant, is trustworthy, and performs in the absence of the master "until the Lord comes" (I Cor 4:5).

The position of servant is meant to deprive the steward of independence and possessiveness. The virtue of trustworthiness points to a reliability, an inner authority that has developed "on the job" and on which both the steward and the community can depend. The third characteristic is more complex and perhaps frightening: the context of this exercise of leadership is absence. The authority of stewards arises both from their trustworthiness and from the absence of their master.

The absence of Jesus Christ, begun in his traumatic death and celebrated in his ascension, is the context of Christian stewardship. In his death Jesus absented himself from the community. "In a short time you will no longer see me" (John 16:16). This loss had startling results: it brought the Spirit into our midst in new and stirring ways, and it lured us into more authoritive roles in our shared life. In the physical presence of Jesus, we had but to follow; we had a leader possessed of God like no other. When the Lord is present, we are all fittingly disciples. In the "generous absence" of Jesus Christ, a space is created, a leadership vacuum generated. The disciples' typical question, "how do we do it around here?" is addressed not directly to Jesus but to his stewards. Jesus' absence invokes our stewardship.

To be sure, Christ is not utterly absent. Because of his continued presence in the Spirit, we remain a community of disciples. But this is not a simple presence that can be expressed in a designated leader's knowledge of God's will for this group. It is a mysterious presence to be attended to and uncovered in a community's prayer and discernment. If we really believe in the ascension and the second coming, we must believe in Christ's absence now, and we must learn to honor that absence. Our participation in the leadership of our community is one of the significant ways that we honor the Lord's generous absence.

But such absence is frightening, and the Christian tradition has been tempted to disguise it. The designation of the community leader as an "other Christ" leads easily to a dichotomy of disciples and master that too hastily fills that absence. The leader, acting in Christ's role as master, announces God's will to the community of disciples. When such a division of followers and leader is rigidified as a dichotomy of laity and clergy, both absence as the context of stewardship and the mutuality of a shared leadership are lost. A rhetoric may then ensue that identifies us all as disciples, but that is likely to disguise the structural sanctions that bring certain disciples to be the decision makers in communities of faith.

Returning to the role of steward in the New Testament, it is important to note its range of nuance. In Luke's Gospel this metaphor of servant leadership describes an ideal of mature responsibility for all followers of Christ. In the Pauline letter to Titus, written at the end of the first century, the term has gained a specific meaning of community leader. The author of this letter has urged Titus to see to the selection of "elders in every town," persons "of irreproachable character; not married more than once" (Titus 1:6). The letter continues with an exacting description of such a person who is to be the steward of the community.

This passage has often been invoked to suggest that the bishop or priest is the unique steward of a community. In a hierarchical vision of the Church, it is quite natural to restrict stewardship and its responsibility to those in hierarchical leadership. Yet, the New Testament allows for a broader, more developmental interpretation of this image of Christian leadership. In *Seasons of Strength* we have pursued an interpretation of stewardship that sees this exercise of leadership as emerging from a matured discipleship.[1] Beginning our religious life as children of God, we mature into "adult children," responsible participants in family decisions. As adult children of God, we merit the name of disciple. Developmentally this stage of maturity is commonly experienced during our twenties and thirties; we are learning, in our adult choices of career and affection, to follow Christ. Here, too, our first attempts to minister to one another develop; discipleship is the first stage of adult Christian faith. But as our vocations mature, increasing responsibilities in job and family invite and compel us to another level of involvement in the community. As we mature as disciples, our new roles of responsibility and leadership demand a new name. Disciples become stewards.

Disciples into Stewards

If this movement of maturing is expected of every Christian, not just of those entering well-defined leadership roles, it becomes necessary to trace this journey of religious maturing. For many the transition happens in the late thirties or early forties. An external event may trigger this change, perhaps an assignment change, in ministry or a promotion in one's responsibility at work. The triggering even may be within the family, as parents realize that it is they who must decide about their children's religious education. Or the impetus toward stewardship may be more interior: I sense I must begin to take my own religious experience more seriously, or I feel the need to be a more active contributor to my community of faith.

Whether the impulse is external or internal, the movement toward stewardship is recognized in a surge of responsibility and personal authority. We find we are called to trust ourselves in new and perhaps frightening ways. Formerly we could turn to others and ask the disciple's question: "How do we do it around here?" Now when this question arises in our community, people turn to us. If we are frightened by this increased responsiblity—"how do I know I will make the right decision?"—we are also consoled by the increasing reliability of our own experience, accumulated and tested over the past several decades. During our years of discipleship, we have been learning how to care well for others, how to express both our affection and our anger, how to act justly. We find that, despite our many weaknesses, we have become more dependable. This increased personal authority and dependability mean that we are now more than followers; we are becoming stewards.

This surge of responsibility and authority is matched by a paradoxical realization: as stewards we are responsible for what we do not own. Invited in midlife into more demanding jobs and more authoritative positions, we are reminded that what we care for—children, schools, parishes, natural resources—we do not own. A steward is, by definition, not an owner. When Christian faith takes root in us, we recognize that creation and all its fruits belong to the Lord. Yet, adult responsibility calls us to be assertive and decisive in our care for this creation. The challenge is to be caring without controlling; to be decisive without becoming possessive. The temptation we experience here is the one that accompanies any investment: when we care deeply for something, we are inclined to try to control it, to possess it. Being a parent can initiate this discipline of stewardship. Gradually, often painfully, parents must come to acknowledge that their children are not, in any final sense, "theirs." They are neither reproductions nor possessions. But it is not only by being a parent that adults are taught the lessons of stewardship. If we are fortunate, we also learn these in our jobs and other "investments." Midlife maturing entails a continuing purification of our care and decisiveness. We become able to sustain our investment in what we do not possess.

This paradox of nonpossessive care has a long tradition among Jews and Christians. It is rooted in our most basic relationship with our Creator. The writer of Psalm 39, impressed with the brevity and fragility of human life, expressed this relationship most powerfully: "I am your guest, and only for a time, a nomad like all my ancestors" (Ps 39:12). This sense of belonging to a world that we do not own becomes, in our better moments, our religious sense of identity. This "guest involvement" describes a Christian steward today: parents discover that they are guest parents; a pastor is always a guest pastor. Every adult performance of responsibility and authority is recognized as a guest performance. That we fail at this more often than we succeed only reminds us that stewardship is an extraordinary ideal demanding a severe maturity.

As we mature into stewardship, our responsibility extends beyond our families and jobs to include the Christian faith itself. More than a child or disciple, the steward is responsible for handing on this faith. Special challenges of stewardship are being felt today in three central areas of Christian life: Scripture, liturgy, and mentoring. An examination of these three areas may help outline the future shape of Christian leadership.

We are all disciples of Scripture. Whatever our education or maturity or ministerial role, we continue throughout our lives to be apprenticed to this sacred and revealing text. Our lives are interpreted by Scripture. Ideally, from childhood on, we are being shaped by the rich images and stories of these texts. Disciples of the Scripture in these ways, we are gradually invited to become stewards of the Scripture as well. A steward assumes a more authoritative attitude toward the sacred text. Responsible for handing on the faith in our communities, we become—necessarily—interpreters of the Scripture. We select certain images from Scripture for special emphasis; we call attention to the contemporary significance of a biblical story that goes beyond its conventional understanding; we arrange passages in an attempt to hand on their revelation more effectively. As stewards, then, we stand in that precarious position of being both interpreted by God's Word and interpreting it.

An important example of contemporary stewardship of Scripture concerns its sexist language. In these sacred stories we find God's people consistently called "the sons of men." The persons of strong faith and remarkable deeds in these stories are most often men. The psalms and prayers seem to imply the believer is always a "he."

A child will hardly notice this masculine preference; a disciple may wonder at it. A steward, in concert with other trustworthy interpreters, begins to change it. This is, of course, dangerous business, for these are sacred texts that we are altering. Yet, the responsibility we experience in ministering to a contemporary world authorizes us to participate in that process of interpretation which has always been a part of handing on God's word. In every age Christians have chosen for emphasis the scriptural passages that will influence their lives; the steward is someone who does so with an experienced sense of caution and confidence.

Guided by our Scriptures, we Christians celebrate God's presence in the liturgy. Here, too, we can trace a maturing of discipleship toward stewardship. As disciples we participate in the Church's worship; we attend the liturgy and follow the lead of the celebrant. Catholics especially have had a severe distinction between disciples and stewards in regard to the Eucharist. The altar railing stood as a clear demarcation between the steward who was "saying Mass" and the disciples in attendance. In many of our churches the altar railing is gone, allowing for greater mobility at the liturgy. Parishioners enter the sanctuary to read the Scriptures; a variety of ministers distributes the Eucharist. With more members of the community sharing in the planning of this sacrament, liturgical stewardship is expanding. Stewards of the liturgy differ from disciples not in excellence, but by their mode of participation. A steward is in someway involved in *initiating* the liturgy by selecting the readings, planning the music, giving the homily, or presiding.

Throughout the Catholic Church more adult believers are coming forward to complement the traditional, sacramental leadership of the ordained priest. In parishes in South America, in a priest's absence, lay leaders celebrate the presence of the Lord in the community. In congregations of women religious, stewards of the community are imaginatively designing communion services and other liturgies in the absence of the traditional chaplain. Small groups of lay Catholics are celebrating the presence of the Lord in their homes, not in defiance but as an expansion of the parish's liturgical life. In all these instances, as well as in the greater sharing of the planning and presiding at parish worship, Christian liturgical stewardship is blossoming.

The changes that this portends in Catholic liturgical practice are great. Without doubt some efforts to reenvision liturgical stewardship will include excess and immaturity. Growth seems seldom to be achieved without some embarrassment and even error along the way. More impressive, however, is the potential maturing of the adult worshipping community as its members come to a more assertive sense of their responsibility and authority regarding this central exercise of their faith.

A third exercise of Christian stewardship that is becoming more recognized and celebrated in Christian life is that of a mentor. Mentoring is a role that is simple to define and most difficult to perform. Such a person fosters the growth of a (usually) younger person. A mentor is one who recognizes in me, often before I do, my own potential; this person encourages me in a certain career or vocation. In its noncontrolling care for the next generation, mentoring reveals itself to be an exercise of stewardship.

If mentoring is an ancient role in human society (at least as ancient as the Greek person named Mentor who was asked to care for the son of Odysseus while Odysseus was away on the original odyssey), it has long remained restricted to and so hidden within certain social roles: parent, employer, novice master, veteran teammate, teacher. Each of these was expected to care for those younger. Only recently has this special mode of adult care been liberated from its restriction to special social roles and recognized as a ministry to which every maturing Christian is called.

The hazard of mentoring arises from its relationship to adult intimacy. The mentor nurtures younger persons but is not their parent. The mentor shares affection with younger persons but is not their lover. The excitement and danger of this relationship are rooted in this location between parent and lover. Mentoring is a third mode of intimacy, with potential both for support and manipulation.

The challenge for the mentor is to care for another's future without seeking to control it. As in any exercise of stewardship, one's own life experience is crucial. Only as we become comfortable with our own hopes and careers, can we clearly separate them from the dreams of a younger person. Without this asceticism about our own life, we tend to visit our unfulfilled dreams on the young. And only as we become comfortable with our own sexuality and the commitments that give it its meaning, can we be clear about our affection for the person who sees us as a mentor.

A specifically Christian awareness of stewardship can purify an exercise of mentoring by reminding us that it is a powerful exercise of servant leadership. Mindful that we are serving the hopes and future of the other person, we can better resist impulses to "use" this person to assuage our frustrated dreams or remedy the lack of affection in our lives. In mentoring we guide and encourage the next generation of Christian faith; we become stewards of the Christian tradition.

Exploring these examples of contemporary stewardship, we begin to recognize a special characteristic of this service. Disciples minister from *within* the Christian tradition; grounded in and shaped by its riches, they share its strengths and graces. Stewards have also the added responsibility to minister *to* the tradition itself. Disciples are still learning about the best of our religious heritage; stewards have matured to the point where they are able to, and need to, care for the worst of our Christian tradition. As disciples of the Church, we begin to care for the wounds of the world. As more experienced stewards, we must also come to care for the wounds of the Church.

Such a stewardship arises from a certain vision of the Church. From our very beginnings we have asserted that we are the Body of Christ. Our Christian Church is both graced with God's enduring presence and bears the wounds and scars of this Body. Because it is human as well as divine, the Church is sinful and immature and grievously wounded. Many of these wounds, such as attitudes toward sexuality, authority, and women, are self-inflicted. They are wounds that have opened in the gap between our high ideals and our halting practice.

Who will minister to these wounds in the body of Christ? Children of God are not strong enough to do so; disciples are not yet sufficiently experienced or hardy enough for the task. Only stewards, tested and strengthened by decades of adult Christian living, are strong enough in faith to take up the task of carefully and patiently binding up the Church's wounds. Such a role demands extraordinary maturity and a deep awareness of one's own woundedness. It is a task that we cannot restrict only to our official leaders. For every maturing believer this is the stuff of Christian stewardship.

If stewardship evokes new strengths in us, it also leads us into special perils. The central temptation that is endemic to this stage of Christian service is possessiveness. Involved in responsible choices and authoritative decisions in the community, stewards may forget they are servants. The community or parish or diocese comes to be seen as "theirs." An arrogant or defensive "I'm in charge here" may replace the more open and listening posture of the true steward. Thus there is the need for the special discipline of this stage of leadership to recall, again and again, that our authority is a guest responsibility, a gift to be exercised for a short time in the service of the Lord.

A second threat to the exercise of stewardship is seen in the Christian leader who is unable to let go. Accustomed to leadership and its perquisites, a steward may find it difficult to give these up, to step aside, to hand over leadership to the next generation. Clinging to the status or protection of their authority, such stewards contend that the next generation is not yet ready for leadership. And, of course, from the sagacious vantage of those of us currently in charge, the next generation is, almost by definition, never ready. They do not have our experience or our savvy or our plain good sense. Worst of all, they are not *us*. But they are the future, and it is in overcoming this temptation of stewardship, in learning to share with the next generation the control of the world that will be theirs more than ours, that our stewardship makes its richest contribution.

If stewardship begins in absence, the Lord's generous absence, it also reaches its fullness in absence. In the final maturing of our ministry, we are invited to be powerful enough to let go, to give away our efforts and ecclesial investments to the future. We follow Christ in this letting go, in entrusting our hopes to a future that we cannot control.

What if this pattern of maturing, from discipleship toward steward, describes not just the development of the priest but of every Christian? What if each of us is called not only to be a disciple, but to be a steward? If stewardship can be seen as an ideal of mid-life Christian maturing, it will compel us to reenvision the shape of community life.

Finally, we do well to recall the developmental context of this stage of religious maturing. In the exercise of stewardship we are not allowed to abandon discipleship; we continue to be followers of Jesus and dependent on the strengths of those around us. And in the complex responsibilities of stewardship we must retain, or recover, the child in us. Stewards fail at this integration when they assume a posture of serious self-importance. The child in us, fully dependent on God and wanting to be playful, would rescue us from this unholy earnestness.

This interplay of child, disciple, and steward within the mature Christian leader also reminds us that leadership is not an individual possession nor an elevation in status. As an exercise of community service, it belongs more to the community than to individuals. With this vision of leadership we come to recognize it as more of a shared duty and a collegial enterprise. If the interplay of child, disciple, and steward can become more persuasive than the static roles of clergy and laity, and of women and men, we may find the authority and energy to fully reenvision the ministry of Christian leadership.

Footnote

1. Evelyn Eaton Whitehead and James D. Whitehead, *Seasons of Strength* (New York: Doubleday, Image, 1986).

4. LITURGY AND EMPOWERMENT

David N. Power, O.M.I.

In her chapter in this volume on leadership and power in a social body, Evelyn Whitehead describes the interaction between the individual goal and the social goal, and between the new factors that emerge in the individual's experience and the traditional forms of life and good. Of a religious group, she says that there has to be a tension between the desire to preserve the truth of the group's original transforming encounter with God and the desire to invite individuals now into a transforming encounter with God.

In the Church the rhetoric of power states that its purpose is to empower the faithful. Its claim is that it gives that interior freedom whereby Christians may live in the world, not tied to selfish needs and pursuits, but moved only by the love of God in their hearts. However, because the Church, too, is subject to the tensions mentioned above, the practice of power within it can readily turn into a corporate social control that cannot tolerate much internal dissent and tends to suppress differentiation of experience. The tension between the preservation of a tradition and the service of individual needs is heightened by a corporate quest for social impact on the surrounding culture and society. It is clear that a body that is not closely knit internally, that does not have clear purposes and values to which its members generally subscribe, cannot have a strong social impact. It is in this respect to the internal network of relations and to the corporate presence of the Church in society that power is given structural and symbolic expression. Since ecclesial tradition is being continually reinterpreted in the light of new experience, and since new experience is interpreted in the light of ecclesial tradition, the realities of power in the Church are in a constant process of change. The Second Vatican Council brought with it a fresh experience of Christian community in its interaction on the horizontal as well as on the vertical axis, and a new sense of openness to the power of God's Word and the presence of the Spirit of the risen Lord. With the change in the experience of being Church, there goes change in the articulation of ecclesial reality, and specifically of the ways in which the power of God is mediated and experienced.

The exercise of power and the use and interpretation of images of power occur in a very special way within the liturgical assembly. What is given there is the sacramental representation of the community's participation in the power of God, through the mediation of Jesus Christ and the Spirit through their effective presence in the Church. As churches today look for new ways in which to be an evangelical presence in a troubled society and for the transforming power of the risen Christ in the lives of their own members, changes are necessarily occurring within the liturgical assembly. Traditional symbols and images of power are being reinterpreted, and new ones are being adopted. While ordination is thought of as the primary liturgy of empowerment in the Church, sight can be lost of the radical mutual empowerment of members that is the more basic expression and reality, as well as the context within which official forms of leadership occur.

This chapter offers six points for consideration. First, something will be said about the images of power and empowerment that reflect the nature of the Church as a community of mutual interaction, engaging all of its members. Second, it will take up the question of the canonization of power in the Church and more particularly of ordination and its liturgy. Third, a word will be said about the influence of cultural models of power on the exercise of power in the Church. Fourth, kerygmatic and charismatic images of power will be compared with those that have their roots in images of the cosmos. Fifth, it will be asked how the power of the weak may be made part of the Church's life through remembrance and recognition. Sixth and finally, something will be said about the empowerment that is taking place in many communities that appear to be marginal to the official structures and liturgies of the Church, but that are vital to the renewal of the apostolic and evangelical life of Christian bodies.

The Power of Being Christian

Evelyn Whitehead notes that leadership and power have to be considered within the broader framework of a network of relations within the social body. In other words power cannot be reduced to the issue of the relation between the formally recognized leader and the rest of the body. On the contrary, official leadership has to be seen in relation to the various ways in which individuals affect one another and in which they affect the corporate reality. As far as the Christian Church is concerned, this is one of the things of which the Second Vatican Council signalled a new awareness.

The principal images of power in the Christian kerygma are the power of God's Word, the Cross of Jesus Christ, the Lordship of the Risen One, and the Spirit who indwells. These images speak not only of a power to which Christians are subject, but of a power that is given to them. Total dependence is expressed in the image of Christ's lordship. The power of the redeemed is expressed in the image of the indwelling Spirit. The nature of power and its presence in the midst of human suffering is signified in the Cross on which humanity is redeemed and refashioned. Compassionate power is proclaimed in the images of the Father's prevenient love for sinners and sufferers. This is a new wisdom, a power that is hidden in powerlessness, the strength and testimony of suffering undertaken for others. It is the power of judgment pronounced against other wisdoms and powers.

A radical sharing in this power is given through the sacraments of initiation. It is celebrated in daily prayer and in the Eucharistic memorial, at the common table of the covenant people. It is a power that reconciles, makes one, and allows the Spirit-filled community to witness in hope to Christ's unique lordship. It is given social and ritual expression in an act of worship in which the Word is heard, the Cross remembered, bread broken and shared, the poor cared for, and prayer uttered in an exercise of a variety of gifts. To be forgiven is to be received by this community. To be loved is to be invited to share at its memorial table. To be sent forth is to go out on mission with its blessing on one's head. To serve is to build up its unity and apostolic fidelity, in a communion of charity with other communities.

Some of the current concern over conferrals of office and recognition of mission springs from the inadequate celebration of this fundamental empowerment, in which all both give and receive. When Church officials restrict certain activities of the faithful in the liturgy to some of the members, they are no doubt prompted by what they see as pastoral concern. However, they risk denying the expression of that power which comes to all the baptized through new birth in Christ and in the Spirit. Some of the canonical rulings on the offices of acolyte and reader are regrettable and actually take away from the full participation of the faithful in the liturgy, the promotion of which was Pope Paul VI's intention in making the rules. It is equally regrettable that the laity's role in ministering the cup or bread at the Eucharist is made to seem like a substitution for priest or deacon, whereas it is better conceived as a normal part of their presence in the assembly.

There are a number of ways in which the baptized empower others in virtue of the gifts of Word and Spirit that they receive when incorporated into Christ and the Church. Here we are concerned directly only with the exercise of this power in prayer and liturgy. Three very good examples are provided by the rites for the initiation of new members into the community, the sacrament of marriage, and the liturgy for the sick.

Since the Second Vatican Council the role of sponsor in the preparation of catechumens has been given fresh importance. The sponsor supports the catechumen in his or her preparation by instruction, by initiation into prayer, by wise counsel, and by upholding the catechumen's desire to live a moral life as demanded by the Gospel. As an integral part of such support, the sponsor has a role in the liturgies that occur in the course of the catechumenate. Sponsors present the candidates, testify to their readiness, and sign them with the sign of the cross in the ceremonies that mark the various stages of catechumenal preparation. These liturgical actions of the sponsors are not empty gestures but sacraments of the empowerment that they give to those whom they sponsor and of the witness that they give to the local community, in virtue of their own participation in the mystery of Christ.

It has long been one of the tenets of Scholastic theology that the two partners themselves are the ministers of the sacrament of marriage and that the priest only takes the role of official witness. Such a position is contested by an Eastern view of marriage which attributes the role of minister of the sacrament to the celebrant of the liturgy. The question is best addressed by choosing neither side but by speaking of marriage as a sacrament celebrated by a Christian community when two persons enter into the marriage union. In such a celebration the president of the assembly and the partners and their sponsors have their respective roles, which, within an assembly of faith, constitute the sacrament of marriage. Since early times, before people spoke of marriage as a sacrament in specific terms, newly wedded couples were expected to present themselves in the assembly, give testimony to their communion in the Lord, and receive the bishop's blessing with the celebration of the Eucharist. In developing a more explicit theology of marriage as a sacrament, it would be well to relate this to the Eucharistic assembly instead of seeing it in terms that include only the couple and the priest. The couple are both empowered by and empower the community. They are empowered by it because they are received as a couple united in Christ, instead of as two distinct individuals, into the Eucharistic mystery. They empower it because by their lives and by their liturgical action they testify to the image of the Eucharistic mystery that is given in their mutual union. The role of a baptized couple in entering into marriage is not a passive one of awaiting a priest's blessing. Nor is it an active one that affects only their relation as two independent persons. It is rather an active one which they exercise as a couple in relation to the baptized and Eucharistic community, to which they give support and service and from which they ask support and blessing.

The third example of ways in which the baptized empower and are empowered by one another is taken from the liturgy of the sick. On the one hand, there is the service that the community renders to the sick person. On the other, there is the service that the sick person renders to the other members in their own vulnerability and weakness. In the daily round the members of the concerned community give physical and moral support to the sick, and the sick who are strengthened in the hope of the risen Lord give support to those who surround them. Such a daily reality has its appropriate liturgical expression in the words and actions that belong in the liturgy and sacrament of the sick, which are genuine acts of mutual empowerment. The community or its representatives surround the sick person in prayer, join him or her in the communion in the Lord's body, pray with and for the person, and support and strengthen by such actions as blessing and laying-on of hands. These are participatory actions in the liturgy, distinct from those of the president of the assembly and exercised in virtue of baptismal priesthood. The sick person also has a liturgical role, not yet adequately recognized in the revised rites for the sick. This is to address the gathered assembly, to testify to it in word or silent action, and to bless its members, collectively or individually. Sickness, however serious, does not deprive the baptized Christian of active powers and ministry. In the faith of Christ, it becomes an occasion when service to the community is rendered in new and distinctive ways. Because of their faith, to which they hold in trial and tribulation, the sick have a ministry of empowerment which may well exceed that of other members.

These examples have been given here, because when we talk of power and empowerment in the Christian community and of rituals of empowering and commissioning, it is important to take cognizance of the images and acts of empowerment that pertain to the role in the liturgy and ministry of the Church of all baptized Christians. It is their neglect that can push us into the position of looking for special acts or rituals of empowerment. The issue of power and its symbolic expression, in other words, cannot be properly addressed unless communities become increasingly aware through celebration of the share in Christ's lordship and Spirit that all their members have in virtue of the sacrament of baptism, and of how they empower one another in various ways by a properly active role in the life and worship of the Church.

Canonization of Power

All power in the Church is a participation in the power of the Word, in the lordship of Jesus Christ, and in the gift of the Spirit. A continuing proclamation of the Word and unity in worship, where Christ is remembered and the Spirit is invoked, are the ways of ensuring that God's power remains present and active in the Church, for the good of its members and the witness of its mission. The proclamation, however, has to be continued in fidelity to the apostolic tradition and the message of the Word has to be adequately interpreted in respect to diverse situations and needs. Likewise, the conditions for unity in worship have to be determined if it is to be maintained. Hence, it becomes necessary to have a canonization of power. That is to say, rules have to be fixed which will guarantee, at least in some measure, the authentic nature of acts of power, as well as ways of supervising the various acts of the community which lay claim to the Word and to the Spirit. The fixing of such rules and the act of supervision become in themselves specific modes in which power is exercised, even to the point of appearing to be the very embodiment of power in the Church.

The first canonization of power is actually the determination of the scriptural canon. Deciding which books are to be taken as the embodiment of God's Word and of the apostolic tradition is to give a point of reference for all life and teaching and to fix the boundaries within which power is to be exercised. Claims to holiness, to authoritative teaching, to sacramental action, to pastoral evangelical leadership, have to offer guarantees that refer to the scriptural canon and can be subjected to judgment on this basis. This is not of course a simple and straightforward process and the laws of interpretation require refinement. Nonetheless, it remains true that in the life of the Church the ultimate appeal that authenticates the presence of power is to the Scriptures.

Hence there is a twofold boundary within which the second canonization of power, namely the conferral of office, occurs. The first boundary is constituted by the apostolic life of the faith community, by which the officeholder is empowered and to which he is a servant. The second boundary is the scriptural canon, of which he is constituted guardian and interpreter, a guardianship and interpretation for which he has to answer to the community.

The nature of this canonical power and its relation to the community is expressed in the ordination liturgy when this is celebrated in due form rather than in the truncated ways that at a point in history became all too common. We can interpret office through the ordination liturgy by taking the following points into account. First, it is celebrated within the Eucharistic assembly, where the Cross of Jesus Christ is remembered and the sacrament of the Body celebrated. Second, the Word of God is invoked as source and origin of all power. Third, the candidate is chosen, or at least approved, by the people. Fourth, the Holy Spirit is invoked as the gift of holiness and the gift of charism. Fifth, the sacral names of priest and hierarchy are avoided, and commonplace names such as presbyter, deacon, and overseer are used.

Since ordination takes place within the Eucharistic assembly, which is the sacrament of the Lord's Body, the Church, it is clear that the ordained do not have power over the Body but within it. The risen Lord is present in the people, who are sanctified in the Spirit, and it is this people which constitute his saving presence in the world. The communion at the one table in the Body and Blood of the Savior is the sacrament of this reality, and all the other sacraments, including that of order, have their significance and meaning in relation to it. Unfortunately, in the course of history, the power of order was verbalized as a power to confect the Lord's presence by changing the bread and wine into Christ's Body and Blood. This meant that it was not understood in relation to the common table. It was spoken of as a power over the sacramental body and over the mystical body, instead of as a service to the one body at the one table, where the Lord is present among his followers and present in them through the power of the life-giving Spirit. Since the liturgical changes inspired by the Second Vatican Council and its memory, the celebration of the Eucharist has become more clearly an invitation to the common table, though much is still lacking in this regard. However, the clearer it becomes that all the people share in the proclaiming of the Lord's Word and in the breaking of the bread, the clearer the nature of the power of order will also become.

Just as at a certain point in history it appeared that the priest had complete power over the sacrament of the Lord's Body, so too it seemed that he had complete power over the Word. The Word of the Scriptures was subordinated in practice to the priestly word. Since those in order were said to be by office the authentic interpreters of the Word, and since they were the only ones who spoke the Word in the Mass, it seemed as though the Church learned of God only through them. The more, however, we implement the liturgical changes of the new order of celebration, and do so with an awareness of the teaching of the Council on Scripture and on charisms and gifts, the less it will seem that the clergy have control over the Word. The assembly gathers under the power of God's Word, to listen to it, to interpret it for one another as well as the people present are able, and to signify their obedience to it in the sacrifice of praise. The more active is the congregation in its use of many gifts of word and of service, the more it can appear that the charisms of the ordained do not eliminate those of others and that all, including them, are under the ultimate authority of God's Word and live only by its power.

The ancient canons of the Church and the ancient homilies of the Church fathers made it clear that the bishop, as president of the community and of the assembly, was to be chosen by the people and then received by ordination into the communion of other churches. At times the people's approval is presented in diplomatic terms, since it is in the interest of good government that the leader have the consent and approval of the people. However, though this is certainly good practice, it was not the basic principle invoked. The heart of the matter was that the nature of episcopal authority could be spelled out only in terms of that of the community of faith.

His service was directed to the growth of the Church in a communion of word and charity, and it was in this communion that God's power and presence were truly manifest.

At a later stage, when presbyters took over the presidency of smaller communities under the supervision of the bishop, it does not seem to have been the custom to take one chosen by the people themselves. Ordination services from that time, however, show that the ordaining bishop was concerned to have the people's approval and acceptance of the candidate. This request for approval remained in the ordinal until 1968, though of course it had been many centuries since it was understood or put into effective practice. Today, it has once again become a canonical and administrative concern to get a popular participation in the choice and approval of candidates for the episcopacy, presbyterate, and diaconate. Sometimes it is done with more heart than at others, and with the kind of floating population that is so common in the twentieth century it is a hard thing to realize. Whatever the difficulties it should be realized that this is essential to defining the nature and boundaries of the power of the ordained. The ordination rite can make that clear, but of course it will not do so unless the congregation, at least through representatives, has had a say in the choice and preparation of the candidate. Otherwise, the moment of the ordination rite when the people are asked to give their applause (which seems to be the growing custom in the United States) is but an outflow of displaced sentiment.

The choice and approval of the people is at the bottom a recognition of the charism of the Spirit bestowed on the candidate and their part in the candidate's preparation a fine-honing of that gift. An active assembly in the ordination rite can make it clear that the Church which lives under the power of the Word also lives by the gifts of the Spirit. While recognizing the presence of the Spirit and its gifts in the persons of the ordained, the community continues to exercise the many other gifts that are bestowed by this same Spirit. The giving of the Spirit to the ordained does not stifle the other gifts. Moreover, the prayer of ordination, since it is an invocation of the Spirit over the candidate not only for the present but for the future, makes it clear that the candidate can exercise ministry only in dependence on a continuing renewal of that gift. Difficult situations, especially those that arise from the presence of unfit priests in the Church, have led both theology and canon law to spell out the nature of the priestly office in the rather narrow terms of sacramental and jurisdictional power. The traditional ordination ceremony belies those definitions. It invokes the Spirit as a gift to be continuously renewed, and it invokes it as one that gives together holiness of life, a spirit of true service, and the gifts necessary to serve the community in the office bestowed. The permanence of ordination cannot be expressed in terms of a state or status that remains unchanged. If there is legitimacy in the concept of permanence, it has to be expressed in terms of a call, where the relationship between the particular gift and the community that is served by it appears to have an irrevocable quality. Only when an ordination is done outside of relation to a community to be served, can it appear to be something that concerns the person of the candidate in some abstract way that allows him to lay claim to powers that are defined in terms other than that of service to a community. An officeholder without a ministry of service is an anomaly. There may be a hundred different ways in which this relationship of service to a community of believers may be realized, but it is an essential part of the office and its power. Fidelity to the Church's liturgical tradition, which means not only the service but all that led up to it, can keep this before our eyes.

A priest ordained for the cult of the divine, and as an oracular intermediary, can of course claim powers and status that do not depend on the community's consent and acceptance. Such a sacral figure takes on a kind of independent status, one that makes him the bridge between the sacred and the profane, with an attunement to the sacred that earns him special respect and reverence. There is no doubt that the priesthood has often been spoken of in this way in the Catholic Church. However, the very titles given to officeholders in the New Testament indicate how inappropriate this way of thinking is. The only special attunement to the holy that the New Testament allows is that of configuration to the Cross of Christ and of obedience to the Gospel in a way of life. Ministers and officers in the community carry secular names, such as overseer, elder, and servant, in order to eliminate the idea that there is a manifestation of the holiness and presence of God in any place other than on the Cross of Jesus Christ, and in the people who are united in the communion and charity of that faith. This is part of the desacralization process of which mention will be made when speaking of sacrifice and images or models of power. The ordination service as revised has reverted from the use of *sacerdos*, introduced into it in the Middle Ages, to the use of *presbyter*, so that now we have regained all three secular titles of bishop, presbyter, and deacon. Not every trace of priestly imagery has disappeared from the service, of course. Nor is this necessary, provided the play on images is apparent, a play whereby it is denoted that the expectations of the sacred bespoken in the priestly are met in the unusual ways of a service to the reality of community in a breaking of bread and a sharing of cup. One fears that at present this is not clear in the rites of anointing and of tradition of instruments.

Whether the power of the minister is seen to be to consecrate the bread and wine, or whether it is seen to be to break the bread and pour out the cup, makes a great difference in how this office is received in the Church. The action of the Eucharist that concentrates on the words of institution as central moment is different from the action that has the communion as its climax. The congregation's participation is quite different in the two congregations, as also is the image of power. When the words of consecration are accentuated as the moment of divine power, the minister stands alone, distinct from the body. When the communion is experienced as the moment of the Lord's presence and transforming power, then the people share in a mutual empowering in the Lord, and the minister's role is clearly a relationship to the body as such and one to be exercised in the midst of all.

The prohibition of women ministers of communion, and the law that controls even the participation of male ministers, is in fact very astute. When the Eucharist is celebrated in such a way as to lead to the shared table, then the ministers at the table are indeed participants in the power of Christ's presence. The kind of social control that intends to uphold the medieval hierarchy cannot tolerate that kind of intrusion. As women become part of both the exercise and the symbolism of ministry and power, it becomes clearer in the community through the intuition of a shared reality that the existing controls impede rather than promote the life of the community. One could indeed say that because women are full participants in the mutual empowerment of the baptized, as this is symbolized in ministering to one another at a shared table, so it is only proper that they share in the presidency role, which relates to this empowerment. The sacralization of the name and image of the ordained minister blinds us to this reality, whereas the secular names, that have both their male and female forms, awaken us to it.

The secular images of service and authority, their conjunction with the remembrance of the servanthood of Christ in incarnation,

death, and the washing of the feet of his disciples, the invocation
of the Spirit who is the giver of all gifts, the approval of the congregation, and the proclamation of the Word, are all ways through
which ordination places the role of the ordained in relation to the
Eucharistic sacrament within which it takes place. They are the acts
and images which symbolize for the Church the nature of the power
given to the ordained and its relation to the power which remains
within the community that is shared by all. They are the things that
give insight into the reasons for and the boundaries of the canonization of power in the Church. They are the starting-point for a
theology of Church office.

Cultural Models

While the primary images of power, those that pertain both to
the baptized and to the ordained, come from the biblical tradition,
it is clear that in the course of history they have been conjoined
with images taken from the contemporary culture and that their
use has been affected by cultural perceptions of society and of
authority. Evelyn Whitehead treats in her chapter some of the current perceptions of authority in Western society and of how Church
leadership is affected by these. In particular she shows how the leader
can be set over against the community in a number of ways and
how the exercise of leadership can be attributed to the few, in ig-
norance of the network of interrelationships within the society as
a whole or of the extent to which a leader simply responds to what
are the social body's expectations.

As she points out, the exercise of power in the Church has always been affected by cultural perceptions, since the Church
community must visualize and name its power in relation to the
ways in which power is envisaged and exercised in the social sphere
and in other contemporary bodies. It is always part of grasping the
particular quality of one thing to see how it relates to and is distinct from others. For the Church it is inevitable that its members
share in the common cultural grasp of what constitutes power and
its exercise. Preaching and liturgy relate to this common grasp in
some way, whatever may be the appeal to particular sources of understanding. The Church may then proceed in one or other of two
ways. It may define its own nature and purpose, particularly its
sense of power, by way of contrast with current models, not con-
forming to the ways of this world, or it can for good policy adopt
these models, modifying them by relating them to the biblical im-

ages and remembrances. A few examples can serve to show how this took place in the past, examples that indeed will show that the current canonical and theological explanations of authority owe their origins not only to the biblical tradition but also to particular moments of the Church's cultural history.

The power that shapes a community may not be immediately associated in contemporary Western society with the practice or notion of sacrifice, but in the history of cultures and religions it is indeed one of the primary images and exercises of power. In the Jewish and Hellenistic societies of early Christian beginnings, sacrifices of various kinds were very important social rituals and an outstanding ritual way whereby to denote the presence of a numinous power in the world. Because of the redemption in the Blood of Jesus Christ, early Christians saw themselves cut off by their beliefs from any sacrificial practice. It was inevitable, however, that they had to take account of this practice and its imagery, first, in order to meet the accusation of being irreligious and second, to relate their own sense of the holy to the cultural models. The initial appropriation of sacrificial imagery was done by way of relating it to ethics and an interior life of faith and evangelical obedience. This was quite a startling procedure, because it implied that divine power was primarily an internal gift, and it manifested itself most of all in the way of living of a community and, hence, not in sacred rituals of the numinous. Since sacrifice was a ritual confided to a priesthood, within a practice of sacrifice the priest or priestess was a person who shared in the power of the numinous manifested in the ritual that she or he had to perform. When the power of sacrifice was located by Christian belief in the community's interior faith and ethical behavior, all the people and not only some of the community's leaders were enriched with the imagery of the priestly.

Such beliefs about the holy naturally found their way into the Christian community's acts of worship. Since these were the daily round of prayer, modelled on Jewish practices and the sacraments of baptism and Eucharist, these activities were enriched by the imagery of sacrifice and priestliness. It was but part of the general persuasion about the holy that no one member of the community could be thought to exercise a priestly power in community worship, since such metaphor could be applied only to the corporate reality and to the life of interior faith expressed ritually and in prayer. Leaders of Christian communities, whether apostles or local ministers, were careful to divest themselves of any claim to power and authority, other than that which they possessed by reason of the Word that they preached and by reason of their participation in the Cross of Christ. Certainly, any suggestion of participating in a numinous sacerdotal and sacrificial power would have been found in flagrant contradiction of the Gospel.

Here, then, we have a good example of how Christians conceived power and holiness in relation to cultural models, not by way of assimilation but by way of contrast and metaphor. It is an example that remains of vital moment to the Church in all ages, because it is one that belongs within the very shaping of the apostolic tradition and kerygma. It is consequently one that has been revived and renewed at various times in the history of the Church, one that is always there to modify other models and to challenge some directions of institutional development. In early centuries its presence in the Church's tradition meant that power was granted in particular ways to martyrs and confessors of the faith, by reason of their witness to the death and resurrection of Jesus Christ. At times this was an embarrassment to those whose power had been given more official forms, but their own power was also subject to the evangelical norms, at least in the sense that their candidacy was thought to rest on a common acknowledgement of their evangelical way of life. From time to time in later centuries, there have been movements which have associated a restructuring of power in the Church with a renewal of the apostolic or evangelical life, that is to say with the fundamental persuasion that the primary way in which God's power is present in the Church has to do with fidelity to the Gospel and its ethic and not with priestly offices or structures.

In the meantime, however, other cultural models of power have had their impact and influence on Christian ways of perceiving divine and ecclesial power and on Church structures. This need not be decried, since it is not otherwise possible for the Church to establish its presence in the world, but it does have to be critically understood, especially in a time of change and renewal.

In and beyond the first millennium various forms of neoplatonism combined with legal ideals of social order to give Christian communities those cultural models to which they related their understanding and assimilation of biblical images and memories. The carefully ordered society of ancient Rome gave an institutional model of good functioning, and neoplatonism supplied the philosophical ideals whereby to give it a solid grounding. While in its apostolic mission the Church continued to preach and foster a life of prayer and Gospel obedience, it related to cultural models of power much more by way of assimilation than by way of contrast, as had been the case in early Christianity. This had its influence both on ways in which the power of God and of Jesus Christ was conceived and imaged, and on ways in which power was shared and exercised within Church structures. The Church in effect adopted a hierarchical vision of cosmic order and took this also as the model for its own inner structure. This meant that the concept of power was developed more strongly in the development and justification of Church office than in the theology of the Christian life and ethical observance. Images and attributions of power, of course, continued to be associated with holiness, but this was much more by way of wonderful manifestations than by way of admiration for a blessed and holy life, lived in evangelical simplicity. In other words, even the holy person was expected to show that his or her life did mean a share in God's power by way of extraordinary deeds, such as healing the sick or controlling devils.

For social purposes, both internal and external, it is necessary for the Church to determine its official and ministerial structures. Theology rightly points to these as channels through which God's grace is communicated. It is also normal that cultural models provide juridical and philosophical understandings that become part of the Church's way of conceiving this mediation. The dialectic with biblical images must continue, however, so that the presence and exercise of God's power in the Church may retain its basis in the gift of the Spirit and the living of an evangelical life. To attach this divine reality solely to office and its exercise is to ignore the biblical foundations of the Christian tradition.

Today, Christians are more conscious of the pluriformity of cultures and of the consequent diversity to be found in the ways in which the Gospel is explained and lived. There is no single universal model that serves the Church in shaping its ecclesial structures and ministries. The one constant that can be asked of any Church, in any part of the world, is that it attends to the desacralizing elements found in the New Testament and that it finds ways of grounding the exercise of power in fidelity to the Gospel and a holy life.

Cosmic Power and the Kerygma

Religious anthropology and the history of religions suggest that there is an initial sense of the sacred and powerful which is given nonverbal expression. Furthermore, these nonverbal expressions enjoy a certain universality across time and cultural boundaries. Symbols of sacred place, sacred person, and sacred action speak of a power that precedes any specific expression of meaning. It is a numinous force that influences human life and cosmic movements and to which the human must pay homage. The good of the human community seems to depend on the respect for this power and on the attunement of human life rhythms to the cosmic and to the life that is in the bowels of the earth. At the same time this sort of religious perspective introduces the distinction between the pure and the impure, relative to the harmony that persons, actions, places, or times seem to keep with the cosmic and divine source of life.

Biblical scholarship acknowledges that this type of religion provides the cultural background to Judeo-Christian revelation, as it also points to a continuing sense of the numinous in elements of the priestly code and of priestly activity. At the same time it points to a break with cosmic religion and its notions of the sacred in the New Testament and in the history of early Christianity. In particular this affected the nature and exercise of authority in the Church. The person of the leader could not be enhanced by images of the sacred, and most specifically by priestly characteristics. Testimony to the Word and to the Spirit and conformity with Christ in his loving service could be the only criteria for the authenticity of claims on authority within the community.

The cultural history of power in the Church shows how at a certain moment the elements of cosmic religion again affected worship and office in the Church and how a revival of priestly images affecting the ordained ministry came about. Current renewal of liturgy and of office is marked by some effort to return to more evangelical perceptions of both. This, however, has brought some disarray and some criticism. For example, critics of recent reforms in Western liturgies complain that they have lost the sense of the holy or the numinous. In common parlance it is often said that the liturgy fails to give the sense of the holy and that priests and religious have become too mundane and democratic. In more sophisticated language the criticism is that liturgy has lost its reverence for cosmic forces and that these are taking their revenge on those who do not know how to relate to them as holy and as signs of the divine ordering of the universe. Ecological and sexual issues are not unrelated to a more radical disrespect for life and to a sense of human autonomy that permits total control of the body and of nature. A reaction, therefore, to change is marked by an effort to bring back the priestly sense of worship and the priestly and sacred images of Church office.

The apostolic and evangelical renewal of the Church, however, is not well served by a revival of images of the sacred that sharpen distinctions between members of the community or that negate the sense of the power that all Christians share by attributing a greater and more holy power to officeholders. The fundamental challenge to Christians is to discover how the Spirit that enlivens each and all of the members brings them into communion with the source of all life in the universe and how it is the same Spirit who animates cosmic forces, history, and the witness of Christian communities.

Inasmuch as the numinous expresses a power that the human community has not fully appropriated, one that is beyond human comprehension and that is the ultimate force at work in the world, it is essential to all worship, including Christian. It is of great importance to see with what rites and with what persons or human relations we associate the discovery of this power, and it is on this score that the New Testament legacy needs to be kept alive and not again subordinated to other cultural images. Christians locate the presence of numinous mystery, of the awesomeness of God, in the sharing of daily bread and in its ritualization and not in bloody sacrifices or in the things that are deemed holy by way of distinction from other things. The power of God is experienced not in the oracular judgment that condemns but in the welcoming forgiveness of a community of love, and it is as much in that forgiveness that Christians extend daily to one another as it is in the rituals of absolution that reconciliation with what is most holy in life is affected. There are no sacred roles that give special access to the holy, but this is open to all in the power of Christ's Blood and in the pouring out of the Spirit. The dialectic of power in the Church is such that, although office is respected for what it signifies and for the unity that it brings to the Church, it is always recognized that the holy person who lives by the Gospel has greater potential in mediating God's love and life than the unholy officeholder. If this is ignored, office and the officeholder are invested with an aura of the sacred that is fearful and overpowering.

The Power of the Weak

In a number of countries today, the most vibrant Christian communities exist among those who are materially and socially weak or marginal. While the action of their ministries is given a measure of recognition by Church authorities, this leaves them dependent on external leaders and without many of the important factors in the life of a Christian community, especially the celebration of the Eucharist. In other parts of the world, where the basic Christian community and social marginalization are not so prominent, there is a comparable awareness of the power that actually exists among those who have always been socially inferior in Church structures, as well as in other social structures. To give place to the effect that this can have on ministry in the Church, it is necessary to attend to a number of the perceptions that we owe to the social sciences and to which Evelyn Whitehead draws attention in her contribution to this book. In particular, quoting Elizabeth Janeway, she has pointed to the participation in the dynamics of social power that belongs to the socially subordinate and to the importance of giving this expression. This is a matter of discovering where the forces that can change the life of a society are located and the attitudes towards their own weakness and suffering that can enable persons to become transforming agents.

While there are passages in the New Testament that retain the sacral name of priest for Jesus Christ, the principal images of his mediation are the taking on of the form of servant, becoming victim, the giving up of his Body, the pouring out of his Blood, the offering of himself in ransom and exchange, and the foolishness of the Cross. These are all images of poverty. It is in poverty and weakness that God's power is made present and transforms the life of the world. Because of his love Christ is reduced to being one without power, to being the plaything of the powerful. This is in Christ the revelation of God's very being, not something accidental to the divine presence in the world. This self-emptying becomes a power for believers in its celebration. It is then appropriated by them as an act which frees, one whose power is in the endowment of freedom. It frees from self-interest as it frees from subordination to the powers of the world and to the principalities and powers that thwart the coming of the reign of God. The Church in its celebration of faith can take hold of the power given to it only when it unites with the commemoration of Christ the commemoration of others who by his grace enjoy similar power.

While the community gathers under the presidency of its ordained ministers, and maintains its communion in respecting their authority, it finds and locates the power of the Spirit in the act of commemorating. In other words, the power that rightly belongs to the ordained is not to be confused with the freeing power that lives in the body. This is exercised in acts of service and testimony that belong in the way that people relate to the world. The early Church was much more adept at keeping this kind of commemoration than we are today. It came to an early realization that its power against evil and its power in the world came from those who in testifying to Christ's name opposed other powers of secular and religious domination. The powerful ones in the Eucharistic assembly of early centuries are the martyrs, whose memory was kept and whose passion narratives were read. Sometimes they were the confessors who had survived persecution. If the power of the martyrs were to be recognized, power could not be denied to confessors, even when it left difficult administrative issues to be solved. What was being recognized was the force of liberation that comes in the Cross of Christ and in the hope of the resurrection. This was not kept as an abstract idea but was given flesh in the death or testimony of those who testified in Christ's name against opposing dominations.

Were each particular Church today to recognize something comparable in the dynamics of its own life and witness, it would be easier to find ways in which to locate the power of ordained ministers within a power that is more fundamental and that has to do with being free from fear and free to testify in word and act. The commemoration of those who in the recent past have given their lives in love and witness, who have in word and deed testified in suffering against cruelty and the forces of annihilation and oppression, is in fact more pertinent to an understanding of God's power in the Church than is ordination.

The cultural models that have affected the Church's own conception and exercise of authority have usually prevented it from giving much recognition to the socially weak, or from allowing the socially weak to have power in the Church's life. The socially weak in society turn out to be the ecclesiastically weak as well. The unlettered, women, children, the handicapped, and the sick have had little to do in determining the flow of Church life, even when, as in the case of women, the Church has relied on them for multiple services to itself and to humanity. What remained historically and theologically unexamined until very recently is the actual impact of women on the life of the Church, or the power that the poor have exercised, for example, in the domain dubbed that of popular religion. The clergy has often been compelled to work with these forces, even to compromise with them, but this has nearly always been in the interst of keeping its own official authority and position.

Within liturgical celebration the power of the socially weak in the Church and in society can be recognized and expressed and thus given its place in a meaningful search for the good of order. As Elizabeth Janeway remarks in her book, *Powers of the Weak,* no good is achieved by romanticizing the virtues of the poor or socially weak. What is to be sought is public recognition of their place in the social order and an articulation of how their presence and activity affects the goals and aims and achievements of society. Such recognition of course affects these goals and aims, since it removes the notion of privilege and disrupts assumptions of hierarchical ordering.

Today it would seem that there is a close connection between the recognition of the weak in the Church and the recognition of the weak in the social order. Believing Christians look to their faith in Christ and in God's kingdom to find the ways in which to affirm their place in the building of human society. As already remarked, it is also often the case that the same people find themselves in a position of inferiority in both Churches and society, because of the way in which Churches share the common cultural assumptions.

When liturgical celebration allows for a shared activity that is based on the assumption of basic equality in the community, this leads to a recognition of the powers of the weak. Not only is this true when a greater variety of ministries and mutual service is given its place in liturgy, but some of the liturgy's most basic symbols relate much more to the socially weak than to the socially powerful. One good example of this is Eucharistic bread.

Eucharistic bread is real bread produced by real people. It is made from wheat sown and grown in the fields, gathered by laborers, milled to flour, baked, and set upon the table. The preparation of Eucharistic hosts and the way in which they appear on the altar has often camouflaged this fact. They appear in such a way that they seem to have no connection with the people, but like vestments and sacred vessels belong to the clerical order. When the bread blessed at the Eucharist is actually produced and provided by the people, when it is spoken of in ways that recognize its provenance, then it becomes clear that there can be no Eucharist without the people who produce the bread. It becomes clear that the blessing of the bread is the blessing of the labors of those who provide by work the basic necessities of human life.

The breaking of the bread and its distribution can be such as to respect its nature and the conditions of its sharing. Some observations have recently been made by Rome decrying the practice whereby people take the bread or the cup themselves from the table. The observations insist that it is proper to the meaning of communion that the Body and the Blood be received from a minister. What is meant is that the minister be either one in clerical orders or a person specially designated. Now it is true that the Body and the Blood are the Lord's gifts, the fruit of the blessing of the bread produced by the people and of the work that produced it. It is bread and work that become the shared property, concern, and communion of the people called in Christ, when it is blessed. This may well be underplayed when people take it from the table themselves. What is shared is by nature received. When one gives bread for the community and its Eucharist, one does not take it back when it is blessed and transformed. One can only receive it back, for it is no longer one's own. However, this does not mean that the breaking and distribution of the bread and the cup has to become a clerical act. If this happens, then the nature of the bread, its production, its being shared, and its blessing is once more camouflaged. It is the bread of the people and for the people. It is the Body of the Lord for the people and shared by the people. The ordained minister is minister to this sharing. The exercise of the ministry is dependent on the bread given by the people and on their willingness to share it.

When the *communitas* of the Christian people is recognized in such a fundamental act as the producing, giving, blessing, and sharing of Eucharistic bread and cup, then the Eucharistic symbolism also speaks to the place that the socially weak have in the ordering of society and of public life. It affects the way in which people make conscious the real, if unrecognized, role that they play in public life and influences the manner of their further participation.

It stands to reason that the way in which the past is remembered by the Church affects the power of the weak in both Church and society. Women are telling tales and writing books about the past that attempt to reclaim the role that other women have had in the past, but that has often gone unnamed and unrecognized. In so many parts of the world, the poor and deprived read the gospels with fresh insights into the blessings of the kingdom preached by Jesus Christ. They see that his companionship with the underprivileged of society was integral to his ministry and message, that it had not a little to do with the vengeance that pursued him to death.

In his lordship they find a symbol of the triumph of the power of the weak over the powers that crush and oppress. They have found their own hope and strength in a fresh reading of the story of the liberation of the Hebrew slaves from Egypt. Their veneration of Mary, who sang the song of the blessings of the weak, takes on forms, as in the devotion to our Lady of Guadalupe, that reinforce their hope. They institute their own feasts and find their own saints and heroes in those people who outside the official structures of Church and state brought the poor to an awareness of their dignity and their strength. They give their own testimony in a struggle for freedom that does not yield before apparently superior forces.

To extend these aspects of remembering, churches may need to develop a whole new calendar of saints. The purpose of canonization and liturgical commemoration is presumably to offer models of holiness and protectors. Canonization serves to define the power of holiness, as it is illustrated in the kind of life which the Church sees as embodying the mystery of Christ and his example. The present official list is largely male and clerical. Women figure in it as martyrs, consecrated virgins, or widows who have become holy in widowhood. It has little place for the married, for the laity, for those who follow the single life in the pursuit of a secular career. The only poor that it recognizes are those who retreated from the world, and it forgets those who led people in a struggle for justice. The forgotten of the Church have yet to be remembered. Their remembrance will lead to a new vision of the power of God in Christian life and in Christian community.

Along with this sensitivity to the powers of the weak, there has to go an innate sense of human vulnerability, for without this we lack true awareness of what is shared in human life. The issue of intimacy has to be faced at this level, and the leader has to guide people in this kind of sharing. Moments of weakness, such as the birth of a newborn child, sickness, imminent death, grief over the departed, are privileged moments of liturgical celebration. Recognition of human dependency and inner personal fragility is essential to such acts as giving and taking in marriage, assuming ministry in a community, sponsoring others in the way of prayer, offering God's forgiveness, consoling in grief, and the like. Liturgical celebration places such experiences of dependency and fragility at the heart of the celebration of grace. In celebrating the blessings of the weak, worship should do nothing that covers over their vulnerability and impotency or the pathos of the compassion of Christ that gives strength to the Christian community in its mutual service and its apostolic witness. The witness of the oppressed, the vulnerable, and the wounded can be accepted as an expression of power within the Christian gathering, because daily, in joy and hope, it keeps memory of the self-emptying of Christ and of the manifestation of God's power in the Cross.

New Ministries—New Structures

In this chapter considerable attention has been given to acts of empowerment, symbols of power, and expressions of power that may not often be considered in connection with leadership, public ministry, and appointment to office in the Church. Their importance in a theology and ordering of ministry and leadership is that they point to the power of God that resides in communities that gather in God's name and is shared among them, and is more fundamental than the official forms of power that come with organization and office. It is only in virtue of a retrieval of this mutual empowering that new structures of officially recognized authority can be developed, whether these touch on ordination to Eucharistic presidency and service or on other kinds of structural leadership.

This seems to be in effect what is taking place in a number of communities that for the moment remain either peripheral to what is officially done or that receive only what is deemed extraordinary recognition of their ways of government. These are communities in which there is a grasp of that task of bringing the Gospel to the world against all other claims to allegiance. They are communities that commit themselves in this faith and hope to the quest for order and justice and the blessedness of the poor. They are communities that find their strength in their unity, in their shared hope, and in the mutual empowerment that goes on between the members.

The ultimate ground of an appeal to be accepted as a leader, in whatever post or ministry, lies not in official recognition or appointment but in the integration of one's witness and service into the life of the community in such a way that it serves and develops mutual empowerment among all and a common sense of life and shared task. A rediscovery of the significance of ordination and other forms of social appointment to ministry depends on this integration.

While churches may give due and necessary attention to forms of leadership and of appointment to office other than the ordained ministry, much in the future of the Church does depend on who are called to ordination, on how they are called, and on the criteria used for making choices of candidates. At present the power of women and the power of the poor do not figure among possible qualifications for ordination. This means that their witness can receive only subordinate and nonsacramental forms of recognition. Perhaps it is only when the underprivileged do come to be accepted, within the living circumstance of believing communities, as candidates for ordination to Eucharistic ministry that the true power of the ordained in the Church will come to light. Only if the power of the world's powerless is fully integrated into the sacramental life of the Church, will the revelation of divine power in the Cross of Christ appear in all its folly and its forcefulness.

References

Fiorenza, Elisabeth Schüssler. *In Memory of Her: A Feminist Theological Reconstruction of Christian Origins.* New York: Crossroad, 1983. Illustrates how women can claim apostolic tradition and the example of Jesus for their own vision of life in the Spirit and of the Church.

O'Meara, Thomas F. *Theology of Ministry.* New York: Paulist, 1983. A cultural study of the development of ministry in the course of history.

Power, David N. *Gifts That Differ: Lay Ministries Established and Unestablished,* 2nd ed. New York: Pueblo, 1985. A study of the place of the laity in the Church's ministry, relating it to contemporary trends, the ecclesiology of the Second Vatican Council, and history.

Provost, James H., ed. *Official Ministry in a New Age.* Washington, D.C.: Canon Law Society of America, Catholic University Press, 1981. Essays by several scholars that explore the situation of official ministries in the Church at a time when major changes are taking place in the practice of ministry.

Schillebeeckx, Edward. *The Church with a Human Face: A New and Expanded Theology of Ministry.* New York: Crossroad, 1985. A hermeneutical examination of the origins and development of the ordained ministry in the Church with reference to current developments and their meaning for ministry.

5. THEOLOGICAL ASSUMPTIONS AND MINISTERIAL STYLE

John Shea

The year is 1968. The scene is a rectory with a gathering of older and younger priests. They have just finished a study day on the sacrament of reconciliation. All the speakers at the day stressed the need for a new theological understanding of sacraments and sin and more creative pastoral practices. This melange of priests broke down predictably. The older ones clustered in the living room; the younger ones huddled around the kitchen table.

One of the older priests suddenly appeared in the kitchen. He threw a small, folded piece of paper on the table. "All the theology you will ever need is on that piece of paper," he said. The living room was silent in anticipation. The paper sat there for what was either ten seconds or an hour. Finally, one of the young priests picked it up and opened it.

On the paper was the telephone number of the chancery office.

What the older priest did not realize was that his joke reflected a whole theological world. Crammed between each digit of that telephone number was an understanding of priesthood and the Church, and beyond that validating perceptions of Christ, God, and salvation. He was not atheological, "just a priest doing his job." He was shot through with theology. Only he did not know it.

His predicament is not solely his own. All ministers live within a theological world they have partially inherited and partially created. There is no ministerial style, action, or policy that is not implicitly validated by theological assumptions. Contrary to the protestations of the most pragmatic among us, there is no theology-free ministry. The option for ministers is between being prisoners of unconscious theological assumptions or free people relatively aware of the theological perceptions that are influencing them. Prisoners are doomed to react; free people can creatively respond, affirming and criticising themselves and their situations.

We will explore this relationship between theology and ministry in three sections. First, we will examine a few procedures for surfacing the operative theology of a minister. In ministerial situations most theology is "under the table." Theological perceptions are influential but usually hidden. Values and strategies are easily talked about and form the content of most ministerial conversations. The underlying faith convictions that ground the values and guide the strategies are usually passed over in silence. Bringing these faith convictions and their theological elaborations into the open serves a double purpose. It reenforces the faith identity of the minister and it allows the ultimate rationale for certain actions to be scrutinized. Explicit theological discussions often result in innovative ministerial policies and practices.

Second, we will pursue the ongoing sources of a minister's theological vision. For most people in ministry, faith convictions seem to be a constant. How the truth of those convictions is experienced and what meanings those convictions suggest change during the life journey. A youth minister recently confessed, "I can't see God in all this." Her conviction is that God is present. Her understanding of that presence and her ability to discern it is not what it once was. Her dilemma is not hers alone. Many of us have held on to faith convictions while the intelligibility of those convictions crumbled. In these situations we often cry out that we are having a faith crisis. But what is more probably going on is a theological shift which often includes a "dark night of the soul" period. Our intuitive, heart-held, gut-based faith is alive; our understanding of it is undergoing change.

James Whitehead's chapter maps two changes that many ministers are experiencing. They are moving from a hierarchical to a mutual image of Church and from a discipleship to a stewardship image of themselves within the Church. In the light of our considerations, two comments should be made about this movement. First, as Whitehead points out, these shifts are not a total disjunction. The positive values of hierarchy and discipleship are not lost in the move.

They are incorporated and integrated into the emerging images. Second, these shifts are on the imaginal level, which forms the basis of perceptions and values. Images are not so much what we see as what we see through. When ministers "look out of" the images of mutuality and stewardship at the complexities of Church and ministry, new theological understandings will emerge. These understandings will eventually work themselves out into new ministerial possibilities. Theological reflection which springs from fundamental images eventually changes the concrete shape of ministry.

Theological change is the name of the contemporary game. But how does a minister's foundational imagination and theology change? There are as many stories as there are ministers. We will not attempt to chart the dynamics of change, to ride the turbulence and calm of the river which is each person's life. We will try to discern the hidden springs which, if all is well, refreshingly flow into the minister's mind and heart. In general a minister's theological vision is strengthened by educational contact with scholars, participation in the sacramental life of the Church and personal prayer, and disciplined reflection on significant experiences. It is these interrelated areas which we want to explore, and through that exploration understand ministers as people whose faith is ever deepening and whose theology is ever changing.

Third, we want to explore the faith convictions and theological understandings which energize ministerial styles. Since the permeating context of ministry is Church, ecclesiology would seem to be a natural starting place. Evelyn Whitehead's rendition of the social-psychological tensions that exist in religious groups suggest some relevant ecclesial categories. The tension that exists within a group that wishes to both preserve the "original transforming encounter with God," yet "invite individuals now into that encounter," will inevitably struggle with the questions of authority and conscience. If designated leadership is always part of the group while also representing the group's relationship to the larger, more inclusive community, the categories of local and universal Church are enduringly relevant. If leadership is always a relational reality struggling to avoid the pitfalls of both paternalism and isolation, the interdependence of ministerial responsibilities that flow from ordination and those that flow from baptism is an obligatory conversation. The empirical, social-psychological analysis acutely raises the ecclesiological questions.

The deeper suggestion of Evelyn Whitehead's paper, and one

that is echoed in the reflections of James Whitehead and those of David Power, is more provocative. Evelyn Whitehead sets all power within religious groups in the context of divine power. Human power is relativized by and participates in divine power. This means that the power which all ministries exercise must be in line with the intent and style of divine salvific power. David Power also moves our minds to the deeper grounding of ecclesial power. "All power in the Church is a participation in the power of the Word, in the lordship of Jesus Christ, and in the gift of the Spirit." James Whitehead reminds us that images of Church as both hierarchial and as mutual "arise from our dual conviction of our God as both transcendent and immanent." We cannot stop at the ecclesial. Salvation, our relationship to God in and through Christ, is the ultimate theological category that validates ministerial activity. Therefore, our reflections in the third and final section of this chapter will be to connect theological understandings of salvation with the ministerial styles captured in the code words presence, discernment, empowerment, and transformation.

Surfacing Theological Assumptions

Belief entails behavior. Everyone has, at one time or another, self-righteously cited the Johannine tirade: "Anyone who says, 'I love God,' but hates his neighbor is a liar" (1 John 4:20). The moral implications of faith convictions are of paramount importance. In fact today, when the "ideological mechanisms" of all thinking are quickly perceived, action has become the touchstone not only of sincerity but of truth. When people can talk impeccable theology for quite peccable reasons (to reenforce their privilege and position), the truth of faith convictions and their theological renditions moves beyond the question of their correspondence to the actual structure of reality to examine the type of life they are capable of inspiring. One of the insights of the ancient world has been revived: the saint is the test of truth.

Another way of putting this is that systematic, spiritual, and moral theology are intimately related. The point where they come together is the actual person, in our case the minister in the local Church. The minister is in a living relationship to God which he or she cultivates in various ways. With the help of the tradition, this relationship is articulated in a number of key statements. These statements not only structure the individual's relationship to God but, by the ever-fascinating process of extrapolation, are perceived to be the way in which God interrelates with all creation. This ultimate relationship to God suffuses all proximate relationships and therefore colors the way they are seen and enacted. Although ministerial training may offer separate courses in systematic, moral, and spiritual theology, integration happens or does not happen the first time a minister walks into a room and begins to talk and act.

Surfacing theological assumptions are making explicit the link between first, faith convictions and their theological elaborations which are grounded in a personal relationship to God and second, the ministerial style they encourage. In theory we could begin at either end of the chain. We could articulate the beliefs and how we understand them and then tease out their behavioral implications. Although this way is logical and teaches consistency, it has some definite drawbacks.

First, it often becomes abstract, devolves into "ought" language, and results in a vague sense of guilt that the Kingdom has not arrived. There seems to be an incurable negativism that develops when we start with belief. We say "God is compassionate," and before we know it, we are deep in a discussion of contemporary narcissism. Beliefs, abstractly considered, lead to ideals which nobody is living up to. Although in this process of surfacing the theological assumptions of ministers, the gap between belief and behavior must be discerned and challenged, it should not be the first item to be examined.

A second drawback in starting with beliefs concerns the distinction between espoused and operative theologies. Christian Catholic ministers belong to a tradition which has a creed (many creeds in fact) to which they are committed. These touchstone truths are summary distillations of the more foundational gospel experience of grace and salvation. At Sunday liturgy the Nicene Creed is recited with great equanimity. All the truths are equally accented in the race toward the "Amen." But inside each individual a sorting out process is going on. Each person is constructing a personal hierarchy of importance. To be part of the tradition is to say "yes" to them all, but to be a distinct individual with a concrete history is to find in one or the other a compelling truth which has the power to integrate most of the others. The remaining convictions of the community which the individual has trouble fitting in are not rejected, but if the truth be known, they are temporarily shelved. All are espoused, but not all are operative, in the sense that they guide perception and action.

When ministers are asked directly to name the faith convictions that are influential in their ministry, the usual response is a prolonged period of silence. The difficulty seems to be on two levels. On the first level they have to sort out their personal appropriation of their faith tradition. To merely cite authoritative sources seems too extrinsic. If it is to be their operative faith and theology, it has to move beyond mere inheritance. On the second level they may know their personal belief system but are not sure how those beliefs influence their ministry. The fear is that there is a radical disjunction in their lives, a bifurcation between belief and behavior. Beliefs may be tenaciously held, but style is dictated by situational pressures and expediency. Beginning with beliefs is an option, but, more often than not, it bogs down the creative processes of theological reflection.

Besides, beginning with action is more fun. It is a type of detective work. The action is related and gradually through a series of gentle probes the convictional, validating base of the action is uncovered. The assumption underlying this investigative procedure is that the person is a hidden unity. The fear that faith and theology are self-enclosed, that they have no energetic impact on the ministerial world of action is misplaced. In the lives of most ministers, faith and theology are more than a motivational backdrop. They are analytic tools and policy guides. One of the liberating effects of surfacing the theological context of ministry is to reveal the faith energy at its center. Ministers are not doing secular work—teaching, counseling, community organizing, administration—in a Church setting. They are people of faith attempting to influence life from a faith perspective. For the veterans of many ministerial wars, this truth is far from obvious.

What are the reflective procedures that are helpful in uncovering the faith basis of ministerial actions? First, probing questions concerning ministerial judgments, perception, and planning will set the reflective, theological process in motion. We need some concrete examples to get the "feel" for it.

A provocative trigger question to help someone look at their ministerial judgments is: "Retrieve a ministerial encounter which you judge to be what ministry is all about." This is a summarized response from a priest who does ministerial training. "I was called in to help in a staff conflict. One of the staff, a lay woman, was very overextended. Besides that, she had some personal problems at home. She was supposed to coordinate the peace and justice efforts for five parishes. She wasn't doing what she said she would do, and she was avoiding all evaluation, pleading personal problems. I was able to help her set some limits and get her back on good footing with the staff. I felt good about the whole thing."

A provacative question to help someone look at their ministerial perceptions is: "What do you see in your situation that you think is significant?" This is a summarized response from a young woman who is a youth minister. "Small dreams. Some of these young people dream tiny. I ask them what they want to do and the girls say, 'Stewardess' and the boys say, 'Something that makes me the most money with the least work.' I don't step on these dreams, but I don't leave them alone either. I try to expand them."

A provacative question to help someone look at their vision of Church is: "What do you really want to do in the Church where you are at?" This is a summarized response from a pastor. "The place was really hurting when I came in. People alienated from the rectory and one another. Good people but at odds with one another and the staff. I hope to reconcile the place. I'm not sure it's going to work. Probably some people will just drift away. Nothing will be healed; people will just separate."

There are two temptations in responding to these initial reports of ministerial experiences. The first is to settle for what has been said. People never say it all the first time; in fact usually they never say what is most important the first time. We need to know more. And, using the distinction between event and interpretation, we need more event and less interpretation. Concrete retrievals are most helpful. When events are remembered concretely, the teller reenters into the experience and the hearer has a better chance for "total" understanding. We need to know the settings and conversations between the priest and the staff and the peace and justice minister. We need to know the settings and conversation of the youth minister and the young people. We need to know the settings and the conversations of the pastor and his disgruntled parishioners. "Tell us more."

The second temptation is to be "other-centered." The purpose of the retrieval is to uncover the theological assumptions of the minister. But the overwhelming tendency of most ministers is to look outward and engage in cultural analysis and strategy sharing. A predictable direction of the first conversation would be to talk about the perils and possibilities of staff development; of the second conversation would be to talk about the banality of the teen culture; of the third conversation would be to talk about the pain of pastoring and the "evaporation" of membership. But our purpose is to uncover the minister's operative faith and theology. So the *second* move of our exploration concerns the question why. Why do you judge that encounter to be what ministry is all about? Why do you think small dreams are significant? Why do you want to bring those people together, why not cut bait and start over?

The first response to the why question is invariably stated in the value-laden language of social-psychological parlance.

"It was good ministry because she came to a sense of herself, got her act together, and lived up to her responsibilities with the other members of the staff."

"Small dreams are bad news for there is no room for growth. They get caught on the surface of life, not doing much more than surviving. They become Mr. and Mrs. Blah."

"If people are going to belong to a community, they have to get along. We have to respect differences. We can't split every time there's a disagreement."

These responses uncover the values of the ministers and point to an extremely important fact of the contemporary ministerial situation: deeply held faith convictions are mediated through value statements which use the language of the humanistic traditions of psychology and sociology. The language that is most available today to ministers to converse on a deeper level than strategy consists of generalized value words: commitment, responsibility, identity, accountability, integrity, generativity, growth, creativity, giftedness, listening, openness, availability, presence, effectiveness, et cetera. This language seems to me to provide a necessary mediating function. In fact one of the crucial concerns of contemporary ministry is the interrelating of the perceptions and languages of social-psychology and theology. It might be helpful to briefly explore this interrelationship.

In 1964 Langdon Gilkey recorded some reflections that cause the heads of most ministers to nod knowingly.

> Thus we read that "the church is one," that "it is the fellowship of love among all those whose Lord is Christ," that it is a community bound "by its fidelity to his Lordship and its love for one another," that it exists wherever the Word is purely preached and heard and the Sacraments duly administered, and so on. One cannot help wondering what possible entity on land or sea is the referent for flattering words. . . . Such descriptions of the nature of the Church make good theological reading, but one closes the book (especially if one then

has to go off to field work among teen-agers) wondering what community in what galaxy has just been described.[1]

The fact is that it is often very difficult to relate theological language to experience. What is less difficult is to describe experiences and events in social-psychological language. Social-psychological language deals with the immediate interactions between persons, cultures, and institutions. What it points to is readily observable, and the language itself is commonly available. Among educated people in the United States, it is the lingua franca for interpreting life.

In the past in the minds of many ministers, theological perceptions and language were in competition with social-psychological perceptions and language. The theologically oriented person might say, "I answered God's call to minister in the Church." The social-psychologically oriented person might respond, "Your exposure to church groups as a child and your strong need for clarity and authority made you gravitate toward ministry." Theology fears that social psychology will be reductionistic, that it will flatten its vertical truths about God into horizontal truths about people and culture. Social psychology fears the vagueness of theological language. Theology makes global statements on the basis of scanty evidence and speaks absolutely about areas of life that need to be explored with nuance. A major thrust of contemporary ministry is to move away from this antagonism into cooperation. All of us who are involved in ministerial training are struggling to find a "both-and" rather than an "either-or" approach between the social sciences and theology. This volume and the entire series in which it appears is such an effort.

We do not have to look far to see this cooperative effort at work. At the conclusion of this chapter I am going to suggest that four styles of contemporary ministry—presence, discernment, empowerment, and transformation—are grounded on theological convictions about divine involvement in human life. But for anyone dealing concretely with life situations, the question immediately arises: what perceptions do these values and styles engender, and how are they practiced? At this point social-psychological description takes over and Evelyn Whitehead's chapter, as well as sections of James Whitehead's, becomes complementary. These faith-grounded styles will be worked out in concrete religious groupings. In order for these styles to be effective, an analysis of the dynamics of groups is needed. Social psychology provides this analysis and suggests the skills that are needed to carry Christian faith into concrete action. What does the style of empowerment generated by divine self-giving look like when it is enacted in groups that are in a developmental process which comprises times of preoccupation with inclusion, power, intimacy, and effectiveness? If as ministers we cannot answer that question, we might as well, as one parishioner put it, "stay in bed."

To return to the process of surfacing theological assumptions, we have suggested that the initial interpretation of experience yields social-psychological perceptions and language, and concludes with generalized values. But in order to do theology, the conversation must move to a *third* step: exploring the convictional grounding of these values. This is often a difficult step for ministers. It is consciousness-expanding, bringing into awareness the ultimate rationale for their judgments, perceptions, and plans. It is the attempt to integrate what looks like practical, common sense responses into a wholistic framework. When this third step is taken and the faith basis persuasively explored, the real influence of faith on ministry is perceived. In order to achieve this consciousness, a new round of "why questions" must be pursued. Why is it a good thing to have control over your life and live up to your commitments? Why is it a bad thing to get caught on the surface of life? Why should people hang in there with one another when it is more comfortable to split?

What emerges from the "persistent why" are bottom line faith convictions. Often these convictions cluster around the areas of what it means to be a Christian or to be Church. The pastor might say, "Because the Church has to be about reconciliation or it will lose its identity." The youth minister will firmly state, "A Christian can't skate through life." The priest will hold that Christians make their situations better by creatively using their powers. But beneath these areas of "Christian" and "Church" the ultimate theological area is lurking. *The final warrant for ministerial action is a conviction about divine activity in human life and an understanding of what that activity is trying to accomplish.* Ministerial action, either consciously or unconsciously, tries to cooperate with grace as it struggles with sin to better the human condition. Images, convictions, and ideas about salvation are the ultimate grounding of ministry. Each of these ministers is working out of assumptions concerning sin and salvation. Theological reflection attempts to uncover these energizing assumptive foundations. In this section a three step reflective procedure has been described: first, questions we asked which aim at identifying significant ministerial judgments, perceptions, and plans; second, why these are judged to be significant is probed; third, the convictional grounding of this significance is examined.

In the last section of this chapter we will unfold some theological understandings about salvation that have become "common coin" in American pastoral circles and how those understandings inform ministerial styles. But for now it is enough to note that the process of uncovering theological assumptions is only the beginning. All the validating theology that is uncovered must eventually be challenged. These challenging procedures are not for the purposes of discrediting. The theology that most ministers work out of is basically sound. The challenges expand the theology, and, so the theory goes, with the theology expanded new ministerial possibilities come into sight. In other words, theological growth occurs by first affirming the values of the existing operative theology and then challenging those values to be more inclusive. But the initial step is a most important one. Faith convictions and theological constructions make a difference on a day-in, day-out basis for general ministerial style and specific ministerial judgments, perceptions, and plans.

Theological Resources in the Life of the Minister

Recently I conducted a day of theological reflection with ministers of all shapes and sizes: youth ministers, pastors, associate pastors, pastoral associates, D.R.E.'s, social action ministers. We employed the method we outlined in the first section of this chapter. We looked at our judgments, perceptions, and plans; explored their importance; and uncovered their hidden theological warrants. In the evaluation session one minister asked, "Could we have done this if we did not have a theological background?" The answer to that simple question is exceeding complex, so, having been well trained, I avoided it. But what it points to is the need for ongoing theological input into the life of the minister. Theological resources are the presuppositions for the ability to do theological reflections.

As I noted above, the telling of a recent incident is a good place to begin our reflection on the theological resources in the life of the minister. The resource person, a college professor in biblical theology, had just explained the influence of apocalyptic expectation in the New Testament Church to a group of ministers on a study day. He waited for questions. When none were forthcoming, he asked one himself, "What do you think of all this?" A D.R.E. replied, "I don't know. I am trying to figure out how to use it."

This story can help us explore the first and most traditional theological resources for ministers, that is contact with the scholar, most often an academically based scholar. The response of the D.R.E. is often viewed by full-time college and seminary teachers as narrow-minded. She is reducing the rich field of knowledge to what she can use. The immediately practical is her sole criterion. At best this is a misguided quest for relevance and at worst ingrained anti-intellectualism.

From another perspective she may be voicing a pedagogical principle that is operative among full-time ministers. Effective theological resources must intersect with existing needs. Most ministers' initial systematic contact with the Christian faith tradition comes in classroom settings. The "knowledge of the faith" is imbibed (or not imbibed) through the standard procedures of reading books, writing papers, and asking questions of experts. Although the pastoral implications of faith knowledge may be spelled out, the knowledge is basically "for knowledge's sake." The first disciplined acquaintance with a tradition is to traverse the territory academically.

But once a person becomes a minister and is engaged in ministerial activity, a different learning style develops, one which is appropriate to a different environment. The academy provides an ambiance and a rationale for historical investigation and comprehensive thinking. The local Church provides an ambiance and rationale for creative action and subsequent reflection and for confronting existential questions with more-or-less illuminating perspectives. For theological input to be effective in the life of an active minister, it must interrelate with personal faith questions or professional needs. This, of course, is not true of all ministers. Many, especially priests, have been so socialized in academic models of learning and speaking that this remains their dominant way of acquiring knowledge. Along with this academic learning comes the penchant to turn the diverse environments of pastoral ministry into miniteaching opportunities. But, in general, most people in ministry screen scholarly input for its impact on their personal faith life or usefulness in their ministerial situation.

This interrelating of personal questions and professional needs with academic theological input can be accidental or part of the learning design. The accidental interrelating usually takes place in various "updating" efforts. Study days, lecture series, and short-term courses deal with contemporary understandings of sacraments, moral theology, Christology, Church, and the like. Ministers attend these educational opportunities and take from them whatever personal and professional resources they can. The overly negative name for this procedure is throwing mud at the wall and seeing what sticks.

When the interrelating is part of the learning design, it builds on the type of reflection we explored in the first section of this paper. The existing theologies of the ministers are uncovered, and the areas where more resources are needed are delineated. Input is given after the questions which have been generated by personal and professional experience have been sharpened. In this situation the possibilities of genuine communication between the academic resource person and the minister are greatly increased. (Since this paper deals with the theology of the minister, we will not investigate the input of the pastoral minister to the academic theologian. Suffice it to say, it ought to be two-way street with heavy traffic in both directions.)

A second resource for the minister's theology is an ongoing participation in the sacramental life of the Church and a personal prayer life. In the first section we described a way of surfacing the guiding faith convictions of the minister and his or her theological elaborations. The impression could be given that faith is a matter of mental certainty. The fact is that the minister, like all people, exists in a living relationship to God. The faith convictions that energize ministerial action are partial articulations of that relationship. Through sacramental participation and personal prayer the minister cultivates the relationship with God and through that relationship the relationship with people. Ministers' faith and theology deepen and change because they are in ongoing contact with the divine reality which faith and theology seek to express and communicate.

Ministers hold certain beliefs and buy into certain theologies out of a complex blend of traditional and personal motives. Initially faith convictions and theological elaborations are an inherited reality. They are espoused out of respect for the Bible and tradition, and are the permeating context of ministry because they constitute the community's ultimate self-understanding. This is a perfectly natural position to be in. To belong to a people, especially a people of great age, is to be an inheritor of a surplus of beliefs. Many of them will be respected for basically extrinsic reasons, because they were part of the community's historical articulation of its faith. Many of them also will become personally integrated. They will be internalized and enter into the faith understanding of the minister, both consciously and unconsciously. Although it is the entire faith inheritance that forms the context of ministry, it is the interiorly appropriated faith that becomes influential in ministerial activity.

Through sacramental participation and prayer inherited faith becomes personally powerful. This is true because it begins to structure the living relationship to God, which is the ultimate energy of ministry. The minister may hold as inherited faith that Jesus is the salvific presence of God. This will be part of the community context of ministry. But if through participation in Eucharist, the minister enters into ritual contact with Christ and begins to respond to the healing of one's own sinfulness, that faith conviction will become more active in ministerial judgments, perceptions, and planning. A minister may hold to the conviction that trust in God is central because Jesus held it to be central. But if through personal prayer trust in God develops and it becomes real and not naive, this faith conviction will change ministerial attitudes and outlooks. The world of ministry is a unified universe. Personal spirituality and theological perspective are tightly tied together.

Prayer and sacraments as sources of theological input for the minister underlines one of the crucial concerns of David Power's chapter. Liturgy is a community activity which, at its best, keeps the people in living contact with the reality that sustains and transforms their lives. The minister participates in this activity and so is in contact with the same reality as the people. This should keep ministerial spirituality from becoming a "God and me" preoccupation. Liturgy should instead constitute a shared dwelling in the ultimate dimension of human life which binds people to one another. If ministers, especially priests, experience liturgy as solidarity and not prerogative, this experience will, as Power has noted, contribute to a foundational sensibility which will influence all relationships. Most importantly, it will sensitize the community to that inescapable ingredient of all relating—power.

This is why it is so important to reform the images of power in the liturgy and inhabit them creatively. David Power's analysis makes the challenge concrete and compelling:

> When the words of consecration are accentuated as the moment of divine power, the minister stands alone, distinct from the body. When the communion is experienced as the moment of the Lord's presence and transforming power, then the people share in a mutual empowering in the Lord, and the minister's role is clearly a relationship to the body as such and one to be exercised in the midst of all.

If Christ is to be effectively lord of our lives, we must allow our inescapable exercise of power to be affirmed and critiqued by the servant leadership he reveals. Our primary contact with Christ is through liturgy, Word, and sacrament. If liturgy just mirrors the existing, taken-for-granted forms of separation and power, we are cut off from our world-transforming source of energy. The images of power within the liturgy must always be to some extent countercultural, if they are going to mediate the reality of God who is always to some extent countercultural. The minister who is influenced by the community liturgy which embodies countercultural images of power will be spurred to reflect critically on his or her use of power.

A third theological resource in the life of the minister is disciplined reflection on experience. An ongoing part of all learning in ministry is such reflection. But the experiences that are usually selected for reflection and appraisal are the practical successes and failures, and the increased learning that is sought is usually of a skill variety. A catechist will reflect on how he tried to implement a lesson plan; a minister of care will process her visit to a hospital patient; a preacher will look at the pluses and minuses of his homiletic effort. Experiences are retrieved and analyzed so future similar situations will be more effective.

But the experiences that provide an opening for theological development are usually of a different caliber. These are experiences where the faith and theology of the minister has been reenforced, jolted, or outright contradicted. In these experiences the assertive posture of the minister is usually reversed. In most ministerial encounters the minister is active. Something has to be done and the minister is about doing it. In experiences that have the potential to touch faith and theology, this dominant posture is usually short-circuited. Something happens which puts the minister on the receiving end of the interaction. The situation is reaching the religious core of the minister. The minister usually goes on as usual. Bluff is the natural response to discombobulation, but the minister knows something has happened on the level of faith and theology.

If there is no reflection on experiences of this type, they simply become part of the lost history of ministry. Unfortunately, this is too often the case. Many ministers are experience rich but wisdom poor. People have invited them into their lives at crucial moments, when they have been staring into the Mystery with horror or celebrating it with joy. But these times have been taken for granted or passed over or relegated to simple categories like "it was good" or "it was bad." If ministerial encounters are to be active elements in faith and theology, there is a need for both depth experiences and depth reflection.

The reflection on depth experiences is most powerful when it has moments of both personal solitude and the company of friends. Personal solitude is needed because the impact of the experience is initially only barely comprehended. In the first moment all that is known is that something happened of significance. In solitude we replay the experience and discern more clearly what has had an impact on us. There can be no depth in human life without solitude. But we also need the company of friends. When they hear our experience told in story form and what we have begun to take from it, they can be our reality factor, by suggesting other interpretations and helping us relate what happened more clearly to our faith and theology. In the present ministerial world support groups of various kinds attempt to help their members integrate significant ministerial encounters into their faith life.

A brief example of how ministerial experience gives input into faith and theology might be helpful. A priest visiting a hospital suggested to a cancer patient that even though we do not understand why some things happen to us, we have to have faith that there is a meaning to it all. The patient replied, "I don't care why it happened. I just want the courage to face it and get through it—no matter if it's death or life." This jolted the priest, and later in solitude and with a reflection group he began to allow the experience to have influence on him. He had always thought that God gave meaning to the meaningless things that happened. Even if no meaning could be discerned, "you just had to have faith it was all working together for good." Providence was at work; sometimes its workings are hidden from human eyes. This theological perspective overflowed into his pastoral practice. He encouraged people to "have faith," which basically meant accepting suffering from God as fitting into a larger plan. Any anger at suffering or seeing it as an undesirable curse he viewed as human and understandable. But basically this attitude belied a lack of faith. It was the clarity and intensity of that one patient's response that pushed him to feel and think in another direction. He began to see God's presence to human life as the courage to face meaninglessness, not the power to deny it. We do not know why some things happen, but perhaps we have to trust in a reality that is present to "dumb suffering" without explaining it. Perhaps the Cross of Christ does not confer meaning and dignity on pain and persecution. Perhaps what the Cross of Christ conveys is courage in the face of abandonment. The search for meaning which is integral to Christian faith may have to be modified to include the power to endure. The priest began to host faith insights along these lines and began to question whether his previous understanding was not a form of control rather than openness, a way of avoiding radical trust. Where he will go with these reflections has yet to be seen, but he is in the process of faith growth and theological change through a sustained reflection on this experience.

The upshot of this sketchy rendition of theological resources in the life of the minister is that ministers are in a constant process of deepening faith and developing theology. Their existing, operative theologies are being affirmed and challenged by scholarly input, personal participation in prayer and sacraments, and disciplined reflection on experience. As ministers' relationships to God are realized more deeply and the theological articulation of those relationships more thoroughly developed, new ministerial possibilities are envisioned. Greater integration of faith and life unfolds into greater creativity and ingenuity in helping the Church live out its ultimate identity in the salvific love of God revealed in Jesus Christ.

Salvation and Ministerial Style

The third section of this chapter deals with the content of faith and theology. In the first section we outlined a few "moves" that help ministers uncover their theological assumptions. This was basically a process orientation, exploring how the social sciences and theology interact in the judgments, perceptions, and plans of ministers. In the second section we examined three major sources which provide theological input into the life of ministers. This was basically a formal analysis, taking note of various resources. But what are some of the theological assumptions that are uncovered when ministers reflect? What are some of the theological insights that are articulated when ministers meet scholars, engage in prayer and sacraments, and systematically retrieve and process their significant experiences? It is time for substance.

It is a widely accepted perception that ministries develop out of the needs of the Church in relation to the signs of the times. Whatever ministries exist are in service to the community of the Church and its mission. The mission of the Church is to witness and to act in accord with the kingdom of God. The kingdom of God is the symbolic code of Jesus Christ for divine salvific activity. This cluster of key words—ministry, Church, community, mission, kingdom, Jesus Christ—can be interpreted and interrelated in myriad ways. But one thing is clear: ministry is a relational activity which gains its identity from its interaction with more foundational realities.

One approach to ministry that follows from its interdependent nature is that it should be considered as a whole before it is divided into diverse functions. This would be a healing alternative to the standard way of considering ministries on the parish level. The standard approach is interface defining. The diverse ministries square off, stare at one another, and ask, "What can I do that you can't do?" This usually leads to turf questions: who is on whose turf; how do the youth minister and the D.R.E. divide the teenagers; what is the role of the permanent deacon in relation to the pastoral associate; does the pastor have a separate turf; or does he haunt everyone's turf? When interface defining dominates the pastoral conversation, the question of the Church's mission and how the joint ministerial effort empowers that mission slides into the background. Given the size of most local Churches, there must be a division of labor. But the overall purpose of ministry itself should provide a unitive vision within which the various ministries target different groups and tasks and cooperate with one another.

Style is a mediating word in ministerial circles. It is lodged between a validating theology on one side and actual skills and concrete situations on the other. For example, hospital ministers often talk about their task in terms of presence. Presence is a style word. On the one hand, presence is validated and encouraged by a theological understanding of divine presence. On the other hand, ministerial presence is actualized in a concrete setting, for example, hospital room 205 with Mrs. Simpson, and specified by certain skills, for example, listening to and responding to the tale of her sickness. As we mentioned earlier and is exemplified in Evelyn Whitehead's chapter, theological convictions and values need social science analysis and skills in order to be embodied in the world.

We have suggested that although there are many areas of theology that inform the diverse ministerial styles and different ministerial actions and policies, the ultimate grounding of ministry is our sense of divine activity in human life. Our further suggestion is that four contemporary styles, garnered from listening to countless stories of ministry, are encapsulated in the code words presence, discernment, empowerment, and transformation. Although these styles are specified in different ways by different ministries, they are the commonly shared orientation of all ministry. Our effort will be to explore the understandings of salvation which provide the warrants for each of these styles.

Presence is a word that is often in the mouths of ministers. Particularly, it is a way men and women describe their ministry to people who are facing inevitable diminishments. In times of sickness and death, divorce and failure, crisis in identity or vocation, the minister is present. From the outside, presence as a style may appear to be an excuse. The practical person in all of us asks, "Presence for what? What was accomplished?" The disconcerting reply on the part of the minister is often, "I was just there. Being there was important." This is not a rationalization. Many people tell ministers how important it was that they were "simply there." There seems to be an importance to sheer companionship with someone who represents the Church. The practical and efficient dimension of the person of the minister often must give way to a sense of affective presence.

When the style of presence is probed, however, more than "mere" presence is revealed. More often than not the minister listened, consoled, and helped in numerous ways. What was conveyed was fidelity to the person in their helplessness. Since most people feel they attract other people because they are strong, witty, attractive, and personable, and when they are none of these things they expect to be alone, they are thankful for the company. The minister is there not only in the good times but when life is collapsing. This understanding of presence is the bridge into the theological vision that encourages it.

Like all creatures ministers can be sacramental presences. We hope that through our presence and words the divine presence will be felt and the divine Word heard. There is a terrible risk of arrogance in all sacramental understandings of ministerial presence. As the Protestant sensibility has constantly pointed out, the line between symbol and idol is thin. James Whitehead has pointed out in this volume that one of the dangers in the image of ministry as stewardship was possessiveness. We arrogate to ourselves the reality we are only asked to tend and care for. Ministers can begin to sound like God, not the real God revealed in Jesus but a distorted fantasy of clairvoyant insight and absolute advice. Yet, at our best we believe that where healing goes on and hope is restored, it is ultimately the work of grace. We have been there, but more than we are was at work. Something greater has arrived for which we are thankful but over which we have little control. This sensitivity urges us to speak of sacramental presence.

Two common ministerial experiences check our tendency toward self-importance and keep this notion of sacramental presence in perspective. First, the more experience we have at being with people, the more we know our ineptitude and sin. When we deal deeply with people, ministerial successes and failures are usually neck and neck. Only the inexperienced speak without humility. Second, when presence does result in healing, it is often not because of our strengths. Our weakness and vulnerability can bring the grace that we fantasize our power and perfection should provide. When the presence of the minister is used by the healing God, it is often a bittersweet experience. If St. Paul is to be believed, vulnerability is one of God's least expected but most often used points of entry into human life. This does not mean that divine activity is only encountered in the failure of human effort. But it does mean that divine and human understandings of what heals are often in conflict.

The religious convictions behind the possible sacramental presence of the minister are often expressed in terms of creation and incarnation. God is the sustaining power of all creation. Creation is not only an act of the past but the present recognition that life is given from beyond itself by the ceaseless gift of breath. God did not create and fade. The artist did not abandon the art but entered into the human fray in Jesus. God in Christ took on the conditions of sinful humanity—humanity terrorized by loss and death and worthlessness—and journeyed the rejected life. These beliefs portray the fidelity of God to all that is human. If these are the salvific understandings that inform ministerial style, the minister will be "there." Everyday ministerial presence is placed in an ultimate context.

Our faith suggests that divine presence is not only nonabandoning but it is also inclusive. It is not a companionship only for the justified or only to those who respond wholeheartedly to it. It is a presence to those who are actively in sin and in the throes of destructiveness. In the Gospels Jesus gathers the outcasts, tax-gatherers, and sinners and eats with them in ritual banquet. But he also dines at the house of Simon the Pharisee and extends to all an invitation to the table. This inclusive symbol he describes as the advent of the kingdom of God. The inclusive presence which Jesus mediates is free but it is not cheap. It does not need previous acts of repentance to be enticed. But once the freely given presence is recognized, it demands response. It is an invitation to repent and change. If this is the divine way, then ministry does not merely seek out the likeable; it pursues the unlikely. It moves toward those caught in addictions and crimes on the one hand and those steeped in self-righteousness and prejudice on the other. If God does not wear blinders, ministerial eyes should try not to blink.

Discernment is a second code word of ministerial style. It carries many connotations. It appears at parish council meetings, retreats, days of reconciliation, spiritual direction sessions, and, if one acquaintance of mine is to be believed, finance meetings. Discernment is a process of listening, judging, and making decisions. It attempts to be sensitive to all the impulses of a situation and to stay with them until the best possibility emerges. On the community level discernment hopes to make difficult decisions without causing division. Since parliamentary decision-making procedures result in winners and losers and in some cases factionalism, discernment is seen to be an appropriate style for a Church that strives for unity within diversity. Discernment is the style that wants a decision that gives life to as many people as possible.

The theological assumption of discernment is that God is not only present but active. This activity of God is understood as a lure to human freedom. God is not intervening to make the choice, nor does the choice come through some divine, interior inspiration, nor is the choice already made in the mind of God and we humans must guess at the eternal plan. As James Whitehead suggests in an earlier chapter, this is the age of mature stewards who must take responsibility. The divine works through the human processes of perception and evaluation. The divine and the human are in a cooperative venture. God has risked creation to the hands of the creature. But the divine continues to offer possibilities which are either seized, partially responded to, or rejected.

We always attempt to discern the divine lure in the context of religious tradition. The Church is a people with a history of responding to divine impulses. When that response has been wholehearted, we say "God speaks," or "God acts." In the life, death, and resurrection of Jesus of Nazareth, God has revealed divine love and intention. We use the story of Jesus as as stethoscope to hear the pulsing of the divine lure. What God did in Jesus, God continues to do within the Church and throughout the world. Through Jesus people moved from alienation to communion, from sin to forgiveness, from destructiveness to creativity, from self-righteous elevation to common human bonding, from numbness to compassion, from helplessness to power, from division to solidarity. God is luring us to these same possibilities today. Discernment is a style that wants to hear the Word of God in the many words of the human condition and respond with creativity and ingenuity.

The third code word for ministerial style is empowerment. This style is a result of the discernment process. Empowerment has a double edge, each of which has been sharpened by the chapters in this book. Its first edge is informed by the historical analysis that James Whitehead outlines. The development of ministries in the Church saw an increasing split between the ordained and the non-ordained, and a corresponding division of ministers and ministered unto. The contemporary sensibility wants to incorporate the values of a mutuality code into the inherited hierarchical framework. It talks of collegiality, joint ventures, shared responsibility. The cynic opines that this move toward shared power and responsibility is the result of a priest shortage. The discerner responds, "Of course, how do you think God works?"

The second edge is the Church-culture interaction that David Power spells out in his chapter. The empowerment style judges that the Church has adopted models of power from the secular movements of the Middle Ages without a sufficient critique of that style from the Gospel message. In our day the officials of the Church quickly critique the abuse of economic and political power in the secular society, and so they should. But if the Church is to be more than the denouncer of other people's oppression, it must deal with its own internal questions of authority and power. If Church communities are to be witness of a redeemed way of living, then we must find ways of using authority and power that reflect the revelation of God that happened in Jesus. The emerging style of empowerment pushes against clerical monopoly and dominance models.

What is the understanding of divine power which undergirds this ministerial style? A few sketchy remarks center around love, compassion, and solidarity. In divine presence love and power always interact. Jesus' twin words for God, king (power) and abba (love), make this partnership clear. God's exercise of power is never for divine glory but for the promotion of the well-being of the creature-creator world. Divine power is displayed in its ability to enter into alien worlds and experience those worlds from the inside and journey with them to new life. This is the reality statement the doctrine of the incarnation seeks to make. Real power is not limited to having effects while maintaining splendid isolation, but involves our capacity to be affected as well—our compassion. This compassion results in solidarity. The well-being of one group or individual cannot be bought at the expense of others. This is why Christ stays on the cross until the end of time. He will not come down until we take him off. But in order to take him off, we have to climb up there with him. The power of God is staying power, the hard-nosed, long-haul capacity to dwell in alienation until it is overcome. As David Power has demonstrated forcefully in this volume, whatever power ministries have, it must be aligned and realigned with divine power. All other power is illusory and, in the final analysis, destructive.

The fourth code word, which is also a result of discernment processes, is transformation. Maintenance will always be a dimension of ministry because life must be nurtured and cared for. But contemporary sensibility focuses on the dynamics of change in persons and systems, both Church systems and secular systems. But the style of transformation often suggests a deeper vision. It connotes radical innovation. It is contrasted with cosmetic touch-ups and window dressing. It wants to address causes rather than symptoms. For persons operating with this style, tinkering with minor problems is wasting time. They see our times in eschatological terms. "The ax is laid to the tree; the fire is at hand." The transformative style is adventuresome. It stresses discontinuity with the past. For many people in ministry, the key transformative factor is precisely the recognition of the power of the poor and weak which David Power explored in his chapter.

The God who energizes the transformative sensitivity of ministry is constantly battling the forces of destruction. Divine presence sustains life and is imaged as breath, but it also transforms life and is imaged as wind. This is the day of the wind. Divine presence is not only a lure, it is also a judgment. It judges the oppressiveness of structures and hearts of the people who maintain those structures. Before this presence solicits human creativity to build a better world, it demands repentance and a statement of new purpose. Divine presence means a people chastened of their egocentric preoccupations and radically open to new possibilities. Ministry which participates in this understanding of God's salvific activity is often called prophetic.

A quick summary might be helpful in concluding this section. God is present to human life as a faithful and inclusive presence. Divine love does not abandon people when they are diminishing or walk away when they are hardened in sin. God is a faithful companion. This presence is actively soliciting human response and so there is a need to discern its intentions. Since God "came out in the open" in Jesus of Nazareth, we use his life as eyeglasses to spy the divine lure in our lives. The power of this divine source which calls to our human powers abhors self-absorption and dominance. All the divine energy is spent on the promotion of love through a compassionate sharing that results in a solidarity among all the diverse creatures. This divine love is constantly struggling against the forces of destruction. These forces are not to be taken lightly. They are embedded in our structures and have secretly and insidiously occupied our hearts. This God is the presuasive pressure to repent and change. If this is the God we are in relationship with and whom we believe in; if fidelity to this God who was revealed in Jesus is the ultimate identity of the Church; if ministry taken as a whole is meant to intensify the identity of the Church so that it can pursue its mission; then the style of this ministry might be characterized as present, discerning, empowering, and transforming.

From this rendition of salvific understandings and ministerial styles, it should be clear that theology solves no problems. Faith and theology name the fight. They articulate the arena of struggle. Ministry must creatively translate the eternal redemptive struggle of God and creation into the contemporary Church and through the Church into the society. In order to do this, it needs the analyses and strategies which the social sciences are able to provide. Also the ministers must be aware of the theological assumptions which influence their activity and be open to the ongoing resources for faith and theology that are available to them. This whole process of interrelating faith, theology, social science, and ministry is for the purpose of creatively engaging in the ongoing creation and transformation of ecclesial and social reality.

Footnote

1. Langdon Gilkey, *How the Church Can Minister to the World without Losing Itself* (New York: Harper & Row, 1964) 33–34.

RITUALS

APPROPRIATE ORDINATION RITES:
A HISTORICAL PERSPECTIVE

David N. Power, O.M.I.

We can understand the ordination rites of any given Church or historical period only in relation to the ways in which ministries were exercised and candidates for ordination were chosen. To be properly valued as a historical source, they have to be interpreted in context.

Attention to the actual exercise of an order and to the process leading to a candidate's choice gives insight into the manner of symbolic functioning. One norm for the interpretation of symbols is stated in the axiom: symbols articulate and transform experience. It demands attention to the interaction between experience and symbol.

This is well illustrated by the way a candidate for ordination is chosen. The ordination ceremony always presents this as a divine call and an intervention of the Holy Spirit. At one stage of the history of ordination, the process had to include either the choice by the people or at least the presentation of the candidate to the people before the ordination. Nowadays, as has been the case for some centuries, this is not required, but candidates are ordained on the recommendation of seminary personnel. The people have no part in the process. Even when the people have no say in the approval or disapproval of an ordinand, presenting him as one called by God is one way to have his ministry accepted, since the community does not wish to oppose a divine initiative. The divine call is understood, however, in a very different way when appeal is made to the charismatic service that he has already given to the community, as well as to the people's testimony to this service. In this case the evidence of a divine call and its acknowledgment by the people is interpreted as an integral part of the office entrusted through ordination.

The fact of the matter is that at any given time a host of circumstances influences the ordering of the Church and the exercise of ministry. The history of ordination rites reflects these varied influences, since ordination is a symbolic way of interpreting events and giving them their place in an understanding of God's activity and grace in the Church. The relation of the ordination service, and thereby of the ministry conferred, to the Church's apostolic origins is of no little consequence in this symbolic process.

It sometimes happens that ordination rites of an earlier epoch continue to be used, even when their relation to a current understanding of office is no longer apparent. The history of ordination rites in the Western Church shows that the solution to this inadequacy was to add new rites and symbols to the old. Hence looking at these ordination rites, we find that the additions are more expressive of how ministry and office were understood and exercised at the time of the innovation of the rite. The operative interpretation of the nature of ministry at any given age is thus that which comes mostly from an interpretation of the latest additions. To see what meaning was given to ordination to the episcopacy or to the presbyterate in Mozarabic, Celtic, or medieval Roman Churches, we can look to the rites of vesting, anointing, and the presentation of insignia or instruments of office. In more recent times the choice of the prayer from the *Apostolic Tradition of Hippolytus* for the ordination of a bishop represents the renewed appreciation of episcopacy as a sacrament, which was given voice in the Second Vatican Council and had practical repercussions in a wider exercise of episcopal collegiality. Similarly the addition of a few lines to the ordination prayer for a presbyter reflects the growing concern for a ministry that would give as much importance to teaching as to sacrament.

Ordination Rites and Their Setting

More needs to be said about the relation between the ritual and the practical realities of ministry. As has already been said, this shows up in the more recent additions to a rite. However, it also needs to be noted that the symbols or images offer different meanings in different settings. This is because of the experiential component of the interaction between experience and symbol in symbolic transformation. To probe this interchange, several examples are presented here.

ORDINATION OF A BISHOP

The image of a bishop given in the prayer from the *Apostolic Tradition* and subsequently used in other contexts or prayers is that of high priest, teacher, and pastor. Let us concentrate here on the meaning given by the image of priesthood, reading it in relation to two different styles of ministry.

In the first case the situation is one in which the bishop is chosen by the people, remains their chief teacher and is the one who presides at community liturgies. In the Eucharist he receives gifts from the people for the care of the poor and for his own sustenance. The liturgy is a liturgy of the people. The offering of gifts is integral to this liturgy and to the realities of community. The teaching role of the bishop is exercised within the Eucharist, both in the explanation of God's Word and in the proclamation of presidential prayers. Indeed the chair is one of the symbols of episcopal office. The bishop is also the one who reconciles sinners with the Lord's table when with community support they have done penance.

In this kind of setting, the imagery of high priesthood is congruent with the sacrificial activity of the people in bringing their gifts. It is likewise joined with the teaching role, whereby the bishop guides the faithful in that offering which is their obedience to the Gospel (see Rom 12:1; 15:16). Old Testament imagery is thus related to New Testament tasks, such as presiding at a liturgy of thanksgiving, teaching, and reconciliation. This is an exercise of metaphorical discourse, which engenders new perception and meaning by relating unlikes in a fresh use of language. Indeed there are some explicit Patristic interpretations of the imagery of priesthood, which set Old Testament and New Testament priesthood in opposition by reason of the difference in task. The primacy of the tasks of teaching and of forgiveness over offering sacrifices is said to be that which constitutes the newness of New Testament priesthood. This goes with the difference between the sacrifices of the two orders, those of the old dispensation being holocausts and other temple offerings, that of the new order being the living sacrifice of the faithful who are redeemed in Christ's Blood.

The same imagery of priesthood suggests a different interpretation of the episcopal office when it is conferred in another way and exercised in another manner. The situation envisaged is one in which the bishop is appointed by a higher authority without consultation of the people. He is sustained either by the generosity of a feudal lord or from the proceeds of Church property. The giving of gifts by the people for the poor or for the clergy has no longer any place in the liturgy, other than by way of stipends or stole fees, looked upon more as compensation for functions performed than as gifts. The bishop's role in teaching is so minimal that one can say to the presbyters that their place is to look after the people and his to look after the priests. He appears among the people only on the occasion of solemn liturgies, such as those of ordination, consecration of churches, the blessing of virgins, and confirmation. In this kind of setting, the contrast between Old Testament priesthood and New Testament priesthood is minimized or even muted, so that the former has preponderance in interpreting the ministry for the Church.

ORDINATION OF A DEACON

The principal image of the office of deacon found in ordination services is the word itself that designates the office, namely, deacon or servant. The deacon's service keeps him close to the person of the bishop, assisting him in his ministry to the Church. In early times this role kept the deacon occupied in the care of the poor and in the overseeing of Church possessions, including the distribution of goods to the needy. His place in the liturgical assembly beside the bishop sprang from his role in daily life and from the close connection already noted between the gifts of the people and the Eucharistic liturgy. In these tasks of service, he could indeed be seen as the representative among the people of the Christ who washed the feet of the disciples at the Last Supper.

In a later era these tasks no longer pertained to deacons, who were left only with the liturgical function of assisting either the bishop or the presbyter. In that kind of situation, the imagery of the levites who assisted the priests of the Old Law seemed more applicable, and the office was seen for what it actually was, that is, purely ornamental, an accessory to the solemnity of certain liturgies. The effort to express new meaning for the diaconate in recent revisions of the ordinal is unsuccessful for the simple reason that there is no clear ministry or office actually exercised to provide the experiential component of symbolic transformation. The experience is either that of a supernumerary in a parish or of a person who could better meet the needs of the people as an ordained presbyter.

LUTHERAN ORDINATIONS

A third example of the relation between ordination rite and ministerial practice can be taken from the Lutheran Churches, with specific reference to the revision of ordination services for use in the United States. The Lutheran Church has two offices, that of bishop and that of pastor. Its service book, however, has only one ordination rite, to be used for ordination to ministry in either office. If the candidate for the episcopacy is already ordained, there is no new ordination but a simple installation in office. The ordination prayer of the *Lutheran Book of Worship* appeals to the lordship of Jesus Christ over the Church which is exercised in the distribution of the gifts of the Spirit, incorporating the biblical text of Eph 4:11. The clear sense of the ordination is that it is an appointment to the ministry of Word and sacrament, in virtue of the lordship over the Church of Jesus Christ and for the building up of the Church in faith.

The symbolic language of this prayer in relation to practice presents both an image of the source of ministry and a comment on distinctions in authority. Ministry is one and has only one source. It is ministry of Word and sacrament and has no source of power other than Jesus Christ. The ordering which distinguishes between bishops and pastors is not put on the same footing as the existence in the Church of a ministry of both Word and sacrament, common in any case to both offices. This ordering appears rather as a practical measure, necessary to the niceties of regulating Church life, perhaps blessed by God, but nonetheless an ecclesiastical distinction rather than a divine one. In this case, then, we see how the reality of a distinction between bishop and pastor is interpreted through symbolic language in a way different from the Roman Catholic liturgy's representation of the distinction between bishop and presbyter.

The Roman Ordinal of the Second Vatican Council

The revised ordinal of the Roman Church that was published in the wake of the Second Vatican Council is a hybrid. For the ordinations of bishop and presbyter, it picks at random among the ordinals of history. It keeps a sense of hierarchy firmly in place, both with regard to the distinction between orders and to the relations between ministers and faithful. The consultation on the worthiness of the candidate is addressed in the case of presbyters only to seminary or other diocesan officials, not to the people.

There is, of course, a new emphasis on the role of the Holy Spirit, since the ceremony accentuates the laying on of hands and the invocation of the Spirit in the ordination prayer. More abundant images of service are accumulated here and there in the service, and due note is taken of the ministry of the Word. However, anointing rites and the bestowal of instruments or insignia of office remain.

The general effect is to suggest a close link between the action of the Holy Spirit and the hierarchical engendering of ministries and ministers. This is not surprising, since nothing has been done to change the procedures whereby candidates are chosen or to transcend the distinction between clergy and laity in favor of the reality of a community served by a diversity of gifts. The service in the Pontifical is more true to experience than would be a more romantic ordinal that would make stronger appeal to evangelical images of service and charism. The Church has in fact an ordination service which corresponds very well to the canonical procedures followed in the choice and preparation of candidates. One hopes that there is indeed an action of the Holy Spirit in this process and in the actual ministry of bishops and priests, who have given themselves in generosity to the service of the Church. Critically, however, one can ask whether the Churches are listening openly enough to the voice of the Spirit or fully discerning its action in their midst.

This kind of discernment and a subsequent change in the modes of ministering can come only from the admission of new procedures. In older times the ordination service could acknowledge an action of the Spirit in the exercise of charisms of service and a continuation of this action in the ordination whereby the person was given office. Such an acknowledgment allowed a place for the intervention of the people, who were the ones to receive the testimony of charism to the Lord's power and presence. New procedures might well allow for a similar vision. It is only from such a factual change, prompted by a discernment of the action of the Spirit, that new ordination services can be properly generated. It is one thing to present the ideal of service to a person who is called to official ministry because of an acknowledged witness and self-gift, of which evidence has already been given. It is another thing to present this ideal of service to a person who is expected to have learnt service in the seclusion of seminary training, with but brief excursions outside its walls. No doubt it is better for him—since we are dealing still only with men—to act on a model of service than on one of hierarchical power, but he has yet to "learn obedience" in the way that Christ did.

The ways of the Spirit within the Church are already evident in those communities without resident presbyters which are well served by Christians who have the gifts of apostolic leadership and loving administration, as well as the gifts of prayer that are needed to lead a community in worship. They have given their testimony, and the Spirit has testified in them. Truth is affirmed not only in the mouth of one witness but in that of the communities who affirm this leadership. It remains for the testimony to find echo in the hearts of those to whom it pertains to affirm the continuity of these Churches with apostolic origins through ordination.

References

For perspectives on the history of ordination rites, consult the following:

Collins, Mary. "The Public Language of Ministry," in James Provost, ed. *Official Ministry in a New Age.* Washington: Canon Law Society of America, 1981, 7–40.

Power, David N. *Gifts That Differ: Lay Ministries Established and Unestablished.* New York: Pueblo, 1985, 71–99.

Power, David N. *Ministers of Christ and His Church.* London: Chapman, 1969.

Porter, H. B. *The Ordination Prayers of the Ancient Western Churches.* London: S.P.C.K., 1967.

Jones, C., Wainwright, G., and Yarnold, E., eds. *The Study of Liturgy.* New York: Oxford University Press, 1978, 289–349.

Warkentin, Marjorie. *Ordination: A Biblical-Historical Overview.* Grand Rapids: Eerdmans, 1982.

GUIDELINES FOR THE DEVELOPMENT OF RITES

David N. Power, O.M.I.

In the chapters in this book, a look has been taken at the historical development of ministry and leadership in the Church and of ordination rites. Through the means of sociological analysis, consideration has been given both to present modes of leadership and to the sociological dimension of more ancient forms. Examples have been given of the emergence of new ministries and of new forms of leadership. Cases have been quoted of communities that through a fuller participation of all their members in ministry are developing new internal structures.

Within this broad context the issue of new forms of ritual celebration is raised. Many respected voices are heard recommending patience in the effort to reformulate a general theology of ministry and in the attempt to expand the ritual celebration of newly discerned charisms or newly functioning modes of leadership. The counsel is well taken, inasmuch as all that is new must be seen in relation to apostolic tradition, and discernment of the Spirit has to be the key to engaging in new ministries, to reshaping community structures, and to celebrating in forms that are both a retrieval and a renewal of an ancient tradition.

However, action is always a necessity, and what is new is not discovered without it. In particular new forms of life and new forms of celebration interact mutually upon one another. Attempts to ritualize the current experience of ministry in various communities do not simply follow upon theological consensus; they help generate such consensus by manifesting, at least in part, the sense of the faithful and by submitting all things to the discernment of faith in the Spirit that takes place in common prayer.

By basing our considerations both on community experience and on theological reflection, is it possible to offer guidelines that would assist local communities in discovering and in making a judgment of faith on new ways of celebrating ministry? Have the foregoing chapters made it possible to suggest these guidelines?

A. Reflections on Leadership

BAPTIZED IN CHRIST AND IN THE SPIRIT

A first conviction is that baptism is the root of every vocation and ministry. Communities of the baptized are communities of mutual service and empowerment, as well as communities of evangelical witness and apostolic action. No Christians enjoy a special attunement to the holy in virtue of office as such, for it is only by the gift of the Spirit that the power to speak or heal or teach or pray is received. It is only in a context where the community is respected as the covenant people and living priesthood, where the charisms and ministries of all are gathered into the common life and liturgy, that the service of leadership can be properly recognized and take on measured forms. Hence, one of the first things that has to be done liturgically is to develop the rites of Christian initiation in such a way that their quality as a baptism in the service of God's kingdom and the community's faith emerges. Only against this background will ordination rites or other liturgies of ministry and leadership develop properly.

LEADERSHIP

Leadership is an exercise of service, not prestige. This conviction, so countercultural and distinctively Christian, can powerfully shape a rite of ordination. A tension inevitably arises between the sociological need to distinguish the leader sufficiently so that the role of guiding the community's power is clear and the evangelical need to keep the leader a minister and servant of the community. Theologically this could be expressed as the tension between the need to recognize the power of the Spirit that grounds the ministry and the office, and the need that the one who presides also be as one who serves at table. With the emphasis on servanthood that was confirmed at the Second Vatican Council, ordination and installation rites have been revised in such a way that they no longer include many of the old rituals of elevation that seemed to place the ordained above the community. Similarly in all liturgies of the Church, the insignia of dignity have been restored to their original form as symbols of ministry. Cathedrals no longer have thrones for the local bishop; the thrones have been replaced by the original article of furniture, namely the chair from which the bishop teaches. In gatherings of bishops, there is no dais to mark the place of a cardinal. Altar rails have been removed from between the Eucharistic table and people, so that liturgical presidents and ministers are one with the congregation that gathers around book and table.

Some, however, feel that this replacement of the ordained within the body of the community is still tenuous. Consequently, communities are still looking for ordination rites that move even further away from models of separation and for liturgical space that retains none of the traces of a community divided between clergy and laity.

Plurality in Leadership

A move in this direction would not come from a change in ordination rites but from their context, and would be recognition of a plural and shared leadership. Aware of the strengths and graces available in a community of faith, some communities have seen the fruits of this sharing. Practically in any parish or local community many different kinds of leadership are demanded, inclusive of managerial, financial, teaching, and liturgical skills. These responsibilities cannot be assumed solely by the pastor or by the body of priests and deacons. When they are shared by other faithful, they do not have to be modelled in vertical fashion, as though the pastor delegated powers to the others. Since the grace of service and leadership, in whatever form, is always rooted in baptismal belonging and the gift of the Spirit, it may be appropriate that any significant assumption of leadership responsibility be given liturgical recognition within the congregation of faith and prayer. That is why a number of communities are experimenting with rites of commissioning or of a blessing of various sorts. Others believe that this could lead to a new form of clericalism and consequently prefer to look for ways in which some coordination appears between community service and leadership on the one hand and liturgical service on the other. For example the service of a catechist in and to the Church as Christ's Body is expressed by the exercise of this service within, as well as outside, the Eucharistic assembly. In like manner financial responsibility in the community is joined with the supervision of the collection made for community needs and for community action at the Sunday liturgy. The present state of things suggests that there is room for experimenting with both forms of recognition, and that we need to be attentive for a while to the effects on communities of these new forms of leadership and of their liturgical recognition. It is not the first time in history that churches have endeavored to integrate forms of service other than that of the ordained into liturgical celebration in ways that recognize them as special gifts of the Spirit, for the building up of the Church and of its apostolic activity.

Besides these public recognitions there is much room for an awareness of how many relatively modest, but often skilled, forms of service relate to the community's liturgy. Some headway has been made with the adult catechumenate, where it has become clear that the roles of sponsor and catechist prepare the catechumen for the celebration of baptism and that the ordained minister does not have to repeat what has been done by them. In a comparable way one might ask whether the spiritual direction given by one baptized to another and the confession of sins that takes place in this context do not constitute both the necessary and adequate preparation for a communal celebration of the sacrament of penance and reconciliation, so that the priest does not have to repeat guidance already given or hear a confession of sins already made before God together with a director. In an age where many women and men have acquired special skills in the direction of others, this sense of the relation of a gathering of two (or more) to the gathering of the whole community can both foster ministries and foster a fuller life of faith.

Vocabulary of Leadership

In renewing rites of ordination, or developing other liturgical forms for the recognition of multiple ministries, the question of image and vocabulary is an important one. Names tell us of our identity and worth and constitute the language of mutual address.

The Second Vatican Council in various documents made some first steps in changing the titles of the ordained, or at least in placing new titles alongside existing ones. Thus it brought out the indications of presidency and overseeing inherent to the title of bishop as it originated in New Testament usage. Likewise, to speak of those ordained to parish and other pastoral ministries, it consistently used the title of presbyter, which is the Greek word for community elder that occurs in New Testament and early Church usage.

On the other hand, it continued to give a certain preference to the name of priest, in speaking of both bishops and presbyters, because it wanted to state the primacy of Eucharistic celebration in the exercise of these orders. In recent times, however, Scripture scholars and theologians are gingerly reminding the Christian community that the designation of leaders as priests received widespread usage only in the third and fourth centuries. The New Testament seems to indicate a deliberate refusal of this title to any member of the community. Only Christ is the high priest of the new covenant, and the unique priesthood of the community is the community reality itself, brought about through being a new creation in the Lord and the Spirit. Thus, it is advisable that any use of the title priest for community leaders, whether in ordination rites or in daily parlance, should be relativized by its reference to the common priesthood of the community, as community of the baptized. In other words, it is the ultimate goal of ministry to build up the living priesthood and sacrifice of a community in faith and evangelical witness, and it is only in relationship to this goal that any use of the title priest can be legitimated.

In any case there is room in ordination services and in the common liturgy to bring other names to the fore. This goes with a change in the forms of Eucharistic celebration or of sacramental reconciliation. Since there is a new accent in these celebrations on the sharing of God's Word, the names of teacher or prophet might well be used for ordained ministry. Since the Eucharist is celebrated again in forms that are closer to the sharing of a common table than were the hieratic celebrations of sacrificial ritual, and since there is some return to the domestic setting of worship, titles having to do with hospitality, the presidency of a table, leadership in prayer, and the service of God's guests would be appropriate.

One title that has been given some prominence in these studies is one that is not only recovered from the New Testament but is also suggested by a contemporary sense of public responsibility. This is the title of steward. Stewardship suggests a human maturing as a requirement for leadership. Some accumulation of adult years of experiencing the commitments of love and work seem necessary for leadership. This, of course, would have an effect on the choice of candidates for ordination and on their preparation.

Furthermore stewardship stresses service *within* the community.

It brings out the point that a leader is answerable both to God and to the community of faith, and that the roots of leadership remain firmly in discipleship.

On the other hand, modern communities are often dubious about the use of another biblical and traditional name for Church leaders, namely, that of shepherd or pastor. This unease seems to spring from the cultural gap between us and the New Testament times. We are prone to see in this imagery the distinction between the shepherd and the flock, or an emphasis on the passivity and even irresponsibility of the people. It is hard to retrieve the sense in which this name accentuated the service and the love that a leader owed to the community in imitation of Christ. In face of possible misunderstanding, it is not necessary to stick tenaciously to old words, but the message can be translated into terms and images that appear more culturally apt.

B. Reflections on Ritual and Celebration

The guidelines for ways of conceiving leadership have already brought out some ideas about appropriate ritual and celebration. However, there is also need for some guidelines addressed more directly to this part of our common experience.

RITUAL AND STORY

At the heart of ritual and of its evolution are the ways of remembering the common story. As in the case of early Eucharistic history, the rituals can be taken from the surrounding religious culture. Thus, early Christian communities drew on the ritual of the Jewish communities at home and in the diaspora. However, because the story of Jesus Christ was at the heart of the celebration, the ritual was modified and developed accordingly. Moreover, it was because this story began to be told in different ways, with differing images and metaphors, that there developed different liturgical families in East and West respectively. The reciprocal action of story and ritual on one another cannot be distinctly gauged; reciprocity, rather than the precedence of one over the other, is the key word to understanding.

When it comes to a discernment of appropriate forms of ritual, it is very useful to look at the relation between the way in which the story is remembered and the shape that rituals take. The aspect of the Christian story that is to the forefront in liturgies of ordination or other ministries is that of the action of the Spirit in the Church, and of the Church's communion with the risen Lord in the witness that it gives to God's presence in human history. The questions of vocabulary already mentioned, therefore, will necessarily have their counterpart in ritual actions. Moreover the memories of each particular community's own story have to merge with the memories of the apostolic story. There has to be place, therefore, in the liturgical celebration of ministries for the recall of these memories and of this particular story, as well as for the hearing of the Gospel and other Scriptures.

THE USE OF SYMBOLS

The word symbol is here understood to designate the things and actions to which prayers and words are joined, these being necessary to the ultimate determination of the symbol's signification. In the current life of the Church, people often seem to be looking for new symbols, due to some disaffection with the traditional ones, which finds them inadequate to the meaningful expression of Christ's mystery and of the life of the Church.

This disaffection touches the ritual of ordination, especially those rites that highlight the separation of minister from people, or the priestly character of the ministerial role, as specified by the power to offer the Eucharistic sacrifice. During the centuries preceding the Second Vatican Council and its liturgical reforms, the ordination rite gave prominence to the anointing of the presbyter's hands and to the transmission of the instruments used in the Sacrifice of the Mass. The theology of priesthood was often based on an explanation of these rites, to the neglect of the traditional laying on of hands. In the revision of ordination rites after the council, the laying on of hands was restored to pride of place in all three ordination services, for bishop, presbyter, and deacon. This action is performed at the moment of the prayer of blessing. However, the additional services of anointing, the tradition of paten and chalice, and the conferring of the power to forgive sins are kept in the ordination of a presbyter. This is a fairly typical liturgical compromise.

Some communities are anxious to find symbols of ministry other than those connected with priestly power for the ordination service. They are also looking for appropriate symbols to use in liturgical services celebrated for the recognition of other ministries or other forms of leadership.

New symbols cannot be created on the basis of an idea or a theory about ministry, with any measure of significance appropriate to liturgy. A school of education may write certificates to give to its graduates, with the understanding that this will serve them as a port of entry to certain kinds of employment. A hotel may give its employees badges that indicate where they belong in its hierarchy of services. Since the purpose of both kinds of institution on these occasions is practical, such symbols serve well enough. In liturgy, however, symbols are intended to represent the element of grace and mystery inherent to celebration, or to the services to which people are designated in the act of worship. They ought to be of a nature to give rise to thought and reflection, and to make the community conscious in thanksgiving of the source of grace and charism, as well as of the community's participation through its ministries in the mystery of Christ's Pasch. Hence, it is inappropriate to choose a symbol that seems to us to express an idea about ministry that we have in mind. The use of badges, certificates, or formal commissionings that describe the office in all too practical a way, seems inappropriate for inclusion in liturgies that celebrate ministry.

Symbols that serve a people's identity, or the identification of services and roles within it, are of such a nature that they appear to be given to it rather than created by it. This is true of all cultural formations of peoples, but it is especially true of the Church, which exists purely in virtue of grace and gift. A community conscious of the need for fresh symbols to express its consciousness of ministry has to learn to look for the symbols, or to listen for the symbols, that are being offered to it in a variety of ways. They come particularly from the wedding of a people's own culture with the traditional Christian and biblical stories of ministry and from the actual experience of the Spirit at work in the community through services and through the people who serve. If they are to perform the symbolic function of transforming experience, they have to be deeply rooted in that experience and be adequate expressions of its meaning.

In some of the ritual celebrations that are offered in the pages that follow, the interest has been to bring such symbols to the fore. Thus, catechists or directors of religious education have the ministry of transmitting God's Word, so it is appropriate that they be entrusted with the book of Scriptures, or that they be blessed with the old gesture of laying the book upon their shoulders (it being hardly functional to give them the book to eat, despite many a biblical story of that nature). In the medieval ordination rites for a presbyter, the symbol that stood out was the transmission of the vessels and the things used in the Sacrifice of the Mass, precisely because this was the action that was to the fore in the exercise of the priestly ministry. Ordination exhortations and commentators could draw on this for the elaboration of priestly life and priestly ministry, and for their significance in the life of the Church. Today, communities are listening to different stories of ministry and sense their transformation through a service rendered with different actions and different accents. A fresh use of symbols in ordination rites will be related to this new experience and to the way in which it is related back to God as its source and to the Church's apostolic foundations. The acceptance of the leader into the community that is to be served, the transmission of the book of the Gospels, the call to lead the community in prayer through some culturally appropriate garment of prayer (such as the shawl in the example given) are examples of ways in which the community's experience of ministry can be symbolized and offered for discernment.

LAYING ON OF HANDS

Nothing, it would seem, can replace the gesture of the laying on of hands to signify the granting of all ministry through the grace of God's Spirit, the subjection of the minister to God's Word and judgment, and the link of each community with the apostolic Church. It is a symbolic action that has both anthropological and biblical roots.

Several things are being discussed today about the use of this action in the prayer for new ministers. First, it is asked whether it is too restrictive to use it only for bishops, presbyters, and deacons. Second, it is asked whether the action should be performed only by the bishop, or by the bishop together with presbyters, as the rubrics for ordination now prescribe. Third, it is asked whether there may not be several ways in which the one basic action can be performed, so that it is adaptable to a diversity of cultural settings.

The third question is the easiest to answer. A laying on of hands can sometimes be done over the head, sometimes on the shoulders. It can be done over a person standing, kneeling, sitting, or even lying on the ground. So much depends on how people in different cultures relate to their bodies, and how their bodies relate to the earth.

The second question has already been answered in practical fashion, in a variety of newly developing customs. Lay representatives, parents, community sponsors of the candidate, or at times the entire membership of the community are in different places invited to join with the bishop who presides at an ordination service in laying hands on the ordained. To the apostolic significance of the bishop's action, there is thus added an action that symbolizes the community's part in the mediation and discernment of charism and office. Objections to this practice are drawn either from historical practice, with the argument that it was never done before (always a weak argument, unless the reasons are carefully examined and thought about), or from the persuasion that it wrongly signifies that the power of ministry comes from the people. Accompanied, however, by gospel reading and prayer, the action does not carry this meaning, for the whole service makes abundantly clear that a believing community sees itself as the Lord's Body only in the affirmation of grace and the origin of all gifts and all power in the Spirit. It is only the community's role in encouraging, fostering, discerning, and receiving the Spirit's gifts into its life that is signified by the union with the bishop in the laying on of hands of other community members.

The first question raises more problems, since it is historically and theologically linked with the existence, in and for the Church, of the sacrament of order. It was so that the nature of this sacrament might stand out clearly that the laying on of hands in the attribution of ministries was restricted to bishop, presbyter, and deacon. It is true, of course, that the action had an abundant use outside this sacrament. It was used in penance and reconciliation, in the anointing of the sick, in prayer over a diversity of people for different reasons, and in the sacraments of initiation. As a very common action, therefore, signifying the source of all power and grace in the Spirit, and joined with the invocation of Christ's name and memory, some feel nowadays that it would be appropriately used in the recognition of forms of leadership other than that of the ordained members of the community. When the use of the gesture is so extended, naturally one has to ask what kind of symbolic action will be used to signify the distinctive nature of the ordained ministry, and to bring out what this sacrament signifies for the very being of the Church. Since this involves the growing theology of ministry, and is linked with an internal restructuring of order, as well as with the hope of some changes in canonical legislation concerning candidature, these guidelines can hardly now go beyond this affirmation.

FORMS OF PRAYER

The Church's prayer is always a blessing of God, in the hope of God's blessing upon it. The believing community, when it draws on the richness of its heritage, has a variety of forms of prayer at its disposal in expressing its relation to God. The most elementary forms of prayer, those made most use of in sacramental celebration, are those of thanksgiving and of supplication. These can be connected with one another in different ways, or woven into a larger celebration at different places. However, to guide us in the act of celebration or in planning liturgies, it is useful to keep two things in mind. First of all, all prayer is rooted in memory. In other words, it springs from the remembrance of God's gracious action in Christ, and from the accompanying recognition of that gracious love still at work in the Church. Second, because of this, thanksgiving has a certain priority over supplication, since it is by its nature the act of prayer in which God's graciousness and saving activity is recognized and received with welcoming heart. In this sense a prayer of petition that is filled with hope and confidence comes out of the act of thanksgiving.

To affirm this root of prayer in memorial, and to point to the relation between thanksgiving and supplication, is not necessarily to determine once and for all the order of liturgical prayer. It is only to say that, whatever the order, this relationship should appear. In practice sometimes a prayer of petition that arises from a deep sense of want or of divine absence may precede the thanksgiving, but out of the possible recognition that goes with the willingness to inhabit grief, a thanksgiving may flow, followed by a more confident petition. What does seem open to question is the procedure that would describe the prayer of petition as the blessing, more or less passing over the thanksgiving, or putting some elements after the petition that encompass thanks for what is asked. This suggests a control over divine grace by the Church, or a controlling of the ways of grace's mediation, to which the Church has no adequate claim. The surprising and ever new ways of the Spirit are best expressed in a thanksgiving that derives both from past memory and from present discernment, and that thus grounds our recourse to God in need and in safety alike.

It is hoped that these guidelines are duly embodied in the rituals that are offered in the following pages, by way of example of what might be done. Since ministry and prayer are so much linked

today to the particularities of each situation, care has been taken
to put the suggested ritual in its imagined setting. We are beyond
the day when one set ritual piece can be properly used, irrespec-
tive of place, time, and situation. These sample liturgies simply suggest ways of going about the celebration of ministries. The three
services for nonordained ministries are more likely to serve as models
for immediate use, since they are not in conflict with any canonical or rubrical prescriptions. In official vocabulary they would be
called paraliturgies. This is a useful phrase, inasmuch as it means
that the service is not tightly controlled. The authors and editors
of this work do not intend to suggest that the service for the ordination of a presbyter that is given here could now be used in any
community. The decisions of Church authority that are now binding do not allow this. However, it is their persuasion that a new
liturgy is needed, given the inadequacies and ambiguities of the
present Roman ordinal. The suggested model may aid the thinking
necessary to come to this point, and it may be of some assistance
to communities in mapping those parts of the current ordinal that
are open to adaptation and creativity.

CELEBRATING THE MINISTRY
OF THE UNORDAINED

Evelyn Eaton Whitehead

There are creative efforts in many places in the Church today to celebrate the movement in ministry of those who are not ordained. We look here at three particular settings in which rites are arising. These are religious congregations of sisters and brothers, parishes actively promoting a sense of shared ministry, and diocesan-based programs of ministry training for lay persons. Our intent is to note what is happening in these community-based efforts, giving special attention to issues of terminology that are relevant across these settings. We then offer specific guidelines and examples for the development of rites.

As parishes become more actively engaged in processes of shared ministry, rites are being developed to acknowledge the diversity of ministers and ministries that now exists. In some places the rite focuses on the formal ministers, the priests, and, often, others who are considered to be members of the parish staff. In many parishes there is a ritual of installation for newly elected members of the parish council and other working commissions. As more and more of the "delivery of services" in the parish is taken over by lay members of the congregation (who now in many parishes are the chief persons who conduct religious education classes, prepare young people and adults for the sacraments, undertake action for social justice, visit the sick and hospitalized, care for the poor, plan the parish liturgy, and foster parish groups for prayer and for mutual support), rites are developed to acknowledge those who devote their time and skill to these parish works. Sometimes these are seen as ministries, sometimes more as volunteer services, but in either case they are recognized as of critical importance to the life of the parish. As might be expected, parish communities differ considerably in the theological and liturgical sophistication they are able to bring to the rites they use to celebrate the ministries among them. But the proliferation of these rites points to their necessity in the sense of the faithful.

Many religious congregations now include among their community celebrations rites of commissioning, both for those who are assuming roles of leadership and service within the congregation and, more broadly, for members involved in diverse ministries. Typically this broader commissioning occurs as members are returning to mission settings after a time of community gathering, for example, a congregational study week or jubilee celebration or renewal of religious vows. The commissioning of those in roles of congregational leadership may be celebrated at these gatherings as well, or as part of the chapter of election.

Ministry training programs for lay persons provide another setting in which considerable effort is being given to the ritual celebration of the emergence of ministry. These programs, many of them established at the diocesan level, offer formal training in theology and related pastoral skills. Typically the program is offered as a series of short-term courses or workshops, planned over a two- or three-year period. Often the sequence includes opportunities for supervised experience in particular ministerial settings. Seldom is the program undertaken as a full-time activity; it is instead designed to accommodate the schedule of adults who have a range of commitments to family and work. Participants in these programs are usually drawn from women and men who are already involved in ministry in some parish or agency setting, typically on a part-time and volunteer basis. Sometimes participation in the program is contingent on sponsorship by a particular parish community, with the sense that the participant will be involved in ministry within that parish both during and after the period of formal training. For some participation in the program is part of a larger life transition into a full-time career in formal ministry, but for many it is seen—by both the participant and the sponsoring parish and training staff—as a more solid grounding for one's continuing participation as a ministerial volunteer. There is a small but growing interest in some areas to expand the vision of these diocesan-based training efforts to include participation by lay persons whose sense of ministry is focused on their vocation in the world more than on explicit activities within the parish.

The rites of recognition and commissioning developed within these diocesan-based programs tend to manifest considerable sophistication. This in part reflects the theological and liturgical competence of the staff and in part the wider range of resources that is often available to a diocesan program.

Terminology

In the development of rites to celebrate the emergence of ministry, terminology is a distinct area of concern. This concern for words manifests some of the underlying tension around lay ministry in the Church today. For some lay ministry points most importantly to the universal call to ministry that flows from baptism and the gifts of the Spirit. Sometimes the term is used in a more limited sense to refer to nonordained persons who are serving in designated roles of ministry. These lay ministers frequently have advanced training and professional competence and function in full-time and paid positions in religious institutions such as parishes, schools, and agencies.

For an increasing number of persons in the conversation, the term lay ministry is itself the problem. It is misleading on both theological and practical grounds. Theologically the lay-clergy distinction is being superseded as ministry is increasingly understood to be not a calling limited to the few but an expectation of all who are members of the Body of Christ. Practically the lay-professional distinction no longer holds as the theological and ministerial training of many nonordained religious workers meets and even surpasses that of many clergy.

Other tensions arise in the distinction between professionals and volunteers and between full-time and part-time ministry. These tensions often coalesce around whether one is paid for one's ministry, but at issue as well are the extent of personal responsibility, the level of commitment, and the degree of competence implied by the terms.

Terminology is at issue again in the naming of the rite. Currently the names used to refer to the rites celebrating the movement of adult Christians into the ministry in the community of faith include graduation, acknowledgment, recognition, deputation, commissioning, installation, and ordination. Which term is used depends to some extent on setting—for example, parish, diocese, or religious congregation—to some extent on theological awareness, and to some extent on the ministerial function being celebrated. Sometimes the words appear to be used loosely, almost as synonyms. But more often the terms are carefully selected, the choice itself reflecting a theology of ministry and an accompanying conviction about the place of lay persons in the ministry of the Church.

The term graduation, borrowed from the academic world, announces the completion of a course of study. As such it makes no real claim on ministry. It is not surprising, then, that this term is only infrequently used in connection with rites that celebrate ministry. When it is used, it is usually in a formal educational setting, such as a seminary program or university sequence developed especially for lay persons. Early on in these academic settings the completion of the program may be marked by a graduation. But even here this language seldom is used for very long. As the educational program develops in more ministerial directions, as is most often the case, the focus of the completion ceremony likewise shifts. Several training programs which originally celebrated the graduation of participants moved after several years to celebrations of recognition or even commissioning.

Rites of acknowledgement, recognition, and deputation are somewhat cautious in their claims, their chief purpose being to *announce publicly*. Rites of acknowledgement, for example, are often brief ceremonies included in the liturgy on a particular Sunday as expressions of public gratitude to those who serve the parish in some ongoing way. The focus is on the *generosity* of that small group of persons whose efforts account for much of what actually goes on in any parish. Rites of recognition usually focus on *particular gifts*. In the parish setting these gifts often come to be recognized as a result of some service that has been done, so the rite of recognition often expresses gratitude as well. But its intent is more to affirm the ways in which individuals in the community are known to be personally gifted for ministry. On occasion the recognition terminology is also used for the rites developed by diocesan training programs. Here the ceremony celebrates the gifts for ministry that participants have displayed and that the program has attempted to develop further through challenge and support. Rites of deputation, terminology sometimes used in regard to the liturgical roles of lector or communion minister, are likewise intended to announce, to present persons publicly to a community. The term carries with it an implicit limitation; those deputized do not act out of their own power but as agents of other persons to whom institutional authority more properly belongs. Thus the sense most frequently conveyed, by both the terminology and the rite, is that these persons will be allowed to function in these designated liturgical roles by way of exception. The ministry is not theirs, for it belongs properly to the deacon/priest, but, in light of the needs of the community and the shortage of manpower, they are granted permission to function in a certain capacity. But the rite neither confers any new power for ministry nor acknowledges the presence of any personal charism or gift.

Rites of commissioning and installation make somewhat more assertive claims for ministry. To be commissioned is to be sent with authority. This has important implications for ministry. In most rites of commissioning, it is the community of faith itself that is celebrated as sending the person forth in ministry. Often it is a representative of the community—the major superior, the pastor, the bishop—who speaks in the rite to announce the community's commissioning. Sometimes the role of this person in the rite seems to waver between being spokesperson for the community and its power and being the hierarchic figure who confers the commission out of his or her own power. Groups that are particularly sensitive to this ambivalence will often include several representatives of the community in the commissioning rite rather than the juridical leader alone. The goal is not to bypass the official leader but to under-score the reality of the community's involvement in the emergence and validation of ministry.

Commissioning rites also celebrate the authority of the minister. Here, again, tensions in ecclesial understanding are visible in litur-gical practice. At issue is where the ministerial authority comes from. Theologians today (see, for example, Thomas Franklin O'Meara's discussion in *Theology of Ministry*) point to at least three interde-pendent sources of ministerial authority: the gifts for service with which the Spirit has graced the person in baptism, the validating call of a particular community of faith, and the confirming recog-nition of those in leadership roles who are charged with nurturing the "good order" of the community. Rites of commissioning in use today differ in their emphasis on these three sources of ministerial authority, some stressing personal charism, some the community's call, some the official recognition by ecclesial authority.

Rites of installation most often appear around conferral of office. Vowed religious celebrate the election or appointment of members to roles of major congregational leadership. In more and more congregations the rites celebrate the installation of a group—usually the major superior and council, sometimes the leadership team—rather than a single person. In the parish such a rite may be developed to welcome a new pastor. Some parishes celebrate the installation of new members of the parish council. In other places there is a rite of installation for members of the parish staff or ministry team.

The understanding in these cases is that the rite marks a movement into a recognized position or role to which both authority and responsibility are formally attached. The person thus installed is understood by self and others to have the *right* to the ministry. Thus installation comes closest, at least in terminology, to ordination in regard to the scope and legitimacy it claims for those whose ministry it celebrates.

ALTERNATIVE 1: ORDINATION OF A PRESBYTER IN A CHURCH CONSTITUTED BY BASIC CHRISTIAN COMMUNITIES

David N. Power, O.M.I.

The ordination takes place during the celebration of the Eucharist. Only those sections of the ritual proper to this occasion are printed here. An actual celebration would of course include appropriate introductory, communion and dismissal rites. Attention to the additional non-verbal dimensions of ritual, such as environment, music, and the processions of ministers and people are presumed.

An assembly of representatives from all the communities in the area gathers. The assembly may take place in the principal assembly place of the area, if such a place exists.

Liturgy of the Word

READING

The reading is taken from the Acts of the Apostles, e.g. 2:1-21; 8:14-25; 13:1-3; 14:19-23; 20:17-38.

RESPONSE: Canticle of Mary (Luke 1:46-55)

COMMUNITY NARRATIVE

A leader from each community tells the story of that community's struggle and of its renewed life in the Spirit through reflection on the gospels, through mutual service, through corporate action, and through the flowering of internal ministries.

GOSPEL

The gospel passage may be chosen from the following: Mark 6:7-13; 8:1-13; 9:33-41; Luke 22:24-34; John 13:1-20.

HOMILY

The homily is given by the ordaining bishop.

PRESENTATION OF CANDIDATE AND REQUEST FOR ORDINATION

Leaders of the basic Christian communities present the candidate to the bishop and make the request for ordination, as they see fit.

The bishop questions the community leaders:

Bishop: Do you agree to accept the ministry and
leadership of *N.*,
aiding him by your counsel,
supporting him by your fortitude?

Leaders: We do agree.

Bishop: Do you agree to forge between yourselves the
bonds of charity,
seeking a common unity under the leadership
of *N.?*

Leaders: We do agree.

Bishop: Do you wish to be guided by him
in the preaching and study of the Word of God
and in the discernment of the work of the Spirit
in your midst?

Leaders: We do so wish.

Bishop: Do you wish to search with him
for the ways of prayer in your communities
and to be guided and supported by him
in the celebration of the liturgy and sacraments
of the Church?

Leaders: We do so wish.

The bishop questions the candidate.

Bishop: Having heard the call of the Spirit,

directed to you by your brothers and sisters in
   the faith,
do you undertake to serve them
in fidelity to the Word of God and the
   movements of the Spirit,
as these guide you all
in the way of faith and of mutual charity?

Candidate: I do so undertake.

Bishop: Do you undertake to listen to their voice;
to take heed when they speak;
to direct, reprove, and guide when necessary;
to be always to them a servant who knows his
   own weakness
and acknowledges no power but the power
   of God?

Candidate: I do so undertake.

Bishop: Do you undertake to guide these communities
within the communion of the one Catholic
   church,
in constant cooperation with your fellow
   presbyters
and with me, your bishop?

Candidate: I do so undertake.

PRAYER OF ORDINATION

The bishop lays hands on the head of the candidate and asks the
assembled presbyters, if any are present, and the leaders of the basic
Christian communities to join him in this act as he prays:

Bishop: God, giver and taker of life,
your church is caught in the struggle to keep your
   very name alive.
When it speaks of the service of Jesus Christ
   to the poor,
of his love for the weak and the suffering,
of his saving death,
it seems but a small voice, drowned out by many
   other voices.
It is torn within by divisions,

and in the turmoil of its own growth
seems to find itself bereft of leaders, pastors,
    and servants.

Yet, O God, in the very time of weakness
we remember how you guided your people of old
by calling a nomad pastor into a strange land,
so that he and his wife Sarah
might be the parents of many children,
and the bearers of your covenant with a
    lost humanity.
We remember how you called the shepherd boy,
    David,
from among the flocks
to be the ruler of a kingdom of justice and peace.
We remember how you called the speechless one,
    Jeremiah,
to give voice to your promise of a new covenant
written on the human heart.

People: For all of this we praise and thank you.

Bishop: We remember also how you inspired the young
        girl, Mary,
to see your hand in the birth of a humble child
    in a humble stable,
amid the beasts of the earth,
and before this wonder
to give praise to your power
in raising up the lowly and the weak of the
    world.

We remember how you sent your Spirit
upon your child Jesus,
driving him forth to bring the good news
    of salvation,
giving sight to the blind,
making the lame to walk,
raising up the very dead from the grave.

People: For all of this we praise and thank you.

Bishop: We remember also your great apostles, Peter and
        Paul,
and the communities of Jerusalem, Antioch,
    Corinth, and Ephesus,

enlivened by the gifts of the Spirit,
some teachers, some prophets, some healers,
some administrators, some table servers,
some hosts, some guests,
all servants of one another and of your glory.

People: For all of this we praise and thank you.

Bishop: For all ages, you have given your Church servants
and ministers:
apostles, prophets, martyrs,
carers of the sick, preachers, healers,
each according to the gifts received and the needs
of your people.

Turning from these memories,
we look with new eyes to the wonder of our
own time:
we see in a new Pentecost the flowering of new
ministries.

From among the weak and powerless of the
world,
you raise up to yourself prophets and teachers.
In those who struggle for justice,
you give your Church its martyrs,
witnesses to the truth and to divine love.
We hear the many voices raised
in teaching, prophesying, praying and praising;
and we see the many hands stretched out
to heal, to lift up, to comfort and sustain,
carrying each other's burdens and upholding a
world.

People: For all of this we praise and thank you.

Bishop: Encouraged by this faith and hope,
we turn to you, O God, in humble supplication.
We ask you to bless your servant N.,
who, in the cry of the people and in the word of
the bishop,
has received the call to ministry.
We ask you to pour out your Spirit upon him,
that he may have the gifts of wisdom and
understanding

to guide your people in the way of truth and
love.

People: Pour out your Spirit, Lord.

Bishop: Grant that he may ever lead them
in the reading of your Word
and in the discernment of your Spirit.
Grant that he may be inspired by the flame of
love
to share the people's struggle against injustice
and to learn from their hope.
Grant that he may have a listening heart,
so that he can lead the people in prayer
and in the celebration of Christ's presence in the
community.

People: Pour out your Spirit, Lord.

Bishop: May he, in his own life,
imitate Christ and be an example of true
discipleship.
May he be supported by your grace and by the
care of the community.

People: Pour out your Spirit, Lord.

Bishop: On your people, also, whom he is to serve,
pour forth your Spirit.
Increase among them the gifts of service,
so that Christ's body may be built up and
renewed
to the glory of your name.
All this we ask you
in the power of the Spirit
and in the invocation of Christ's name, for:

All: Through him and with him and in him,
is to you, almighty Father,
all honor and glory,
in the unity of the Holy Spirit,
forever and ever.
Amen.

Presentation and Preparation of the Gifts

The bishop invites the newly ordained presbyter to join him at the Eucharistic table, to receive with him the gifts of bread and wine and the other gifts that are presented by members from each of the basic Christian communities.

The bishop takes the bread and wine and gives them to the presbyter, saying:

Bishop: Take this bread and wine from the hands of the
     people
   whom you are called to serve.
   Know no other gifts than those
   which come to you from God's people and
     Christ's servants.
   Bless God with them for these gifts of creation
     and for the gifts of redemption,
      so that in the communion of the one bread
       and wine
     all may be united
     in the communion of the body and blood
      of the Lord.

The bishop takes the other gifts, such as fruit, milk products, olives, according to climate and season, and he gives them to the presbyter, saying:

Bishop: Take these offerings which the people bring to
     you.
   Share their lives of toil and their joys.
   Be one with them in all their struggles and hopes.
   Bless God in their name for the gifts of the earth
   and the gifts of service that flourish among them,
   so that God's name may be ever glorified.

These gifts are then placed on the Eucharistic table, along with the bread and wine of the Eucharist.

Eucharistic Prayer

The Eucharistic Prayer is taken from *The Apostolic Tradition of Hippolytus.*

Presentation of the Instruments of Office

After communion, the bishop presents the new presbyter with the instruments of his office named below, saying:

Having received the blessing of God and of the
  Church,
given in my person and in the person of those
  whom you are to serve,
go forth from here strong in the power of the
  Spirit
and in the strength of family communion
offered to you by these people.

Giving him a staff:

Take this staff for your journey.
Be ready always to hear the call of the people
  when your services are needed.
Be present among them as an apostle and
  preacher of the Word,
journeying among them as the Gospel demands,
resting among them in the peace that is given to
  you
as you visit their homes.

Giving him a book of the Gospels:

Minister among this people in fidelity to the Word
  of Christ,
showing not only in your speech but in your life
what it is to be a faithful disciple of Jesus Christ,
breaking for them the bread of the Word
and listening to the Word that comes back to you
  from their mouths.

Giving him a prayer shawl:

Don this mantle
as you lead this people in thanks and supplication
  to God.
Let it be a sign for you
that you can speak to the Lord
only if God gives to you the grace of a prophet
and the wisdom of an elder.

ALTERNATIVE 2: BLESSING OF PROVINCIAL LEADERS IN A RELIGIOUS COMMUNITY

Evelyn Eaton Whitehead and
David N. Power, O.M.I.

This ritual should be read as an outline of structures and notes rather than a fixed form. Religious communities differ significantly in charism. Therefore, particular communities would want to select and compose actual texts in the light of their own proper vocabulary and interpretation of leadership within the community.

Call to Prayer

Liturgy of the Word

READING: Isa 49:1-7

READING: Rom 10:13-15

GOSPEL: John 15:1-8

HOMILY OR MEDITATION

A homily is given by a member of the congregation; or a brief meditation, accompanied by sacred dance or slides, invites remembrance of the congregation's history and charism.

Rite of Blessing

THANKSGIVING

The community gives thanks for the diversity of its gifts for ministry in these or similar words expressive of its own charism:

Leader: Just as each of us has one body with many
members,
and not all the members have the same function,

All: So too we, though many,
are one body in Christ
and individually members of one another.

Leader: We have a rich inheritance
in the history of our congregation,
and among us have gifts that differ

All: According to the favor bestowed on each of us.

Leader: One who is a teacher should use her gift to teach,
one with the power of exhortation should exhort.

All: She who gives alms should do so generously.

Leader: She who rules should exercise authority with care.

All: She who performs works of mercy should do so
carefully.

Leader: For all these graces,
that have so abundantly served us
and that continue to be given to us
in the love of the Spirit,
we praise and thank God,
from whom we have received such favors.

All: In the measure in which Christ has bestowed gifts
upon us,
so do we raise our voices in thanksgiving
to the God of light and life.

Leader: For it is Christ who gave apostles, prophets,
pastors, teachers, evangelists
in roles of service to build up the body of Christ.

All: May we continue in our service
to the glory of God's name,
until we become one in faith
and in the wisdom that surpasses all
understanding.

At this point a major superior or presiding sister recalls the connection between baptism, religious profession, and ministry, in words such as the following:

In baptism we have been called forth by the Spirit
to proclaim the good news of salvation.
As missioners of God's love,
we have promised to live in simplicity of life,
in community with one another,
and in the pursuit of the reign of God among all
      humankind.

PETITION FOR BLESSING OF THE PROVINCIAL SUPERIOR

The newly elected superior asks the community's blessing, which is given as follows or in words expressive of the community's interpretation of her role.

New Superior:

    Sisters,
    I ask you to pray for me to the Lord our God.

Sisters: God, our Mother and Father,
    we ask you,
    in fidelity to the promises and the covenant we
      have recalled,
    to bless Sister *N.*

    By the power of your Spirit,
    give her the wisdom and courage
    to be a focus of unity
    and a leader in serving the Christian community.

    This is the ministry
    to which in your name we have called her.
    May she in turn call us forth
    to continue your work in this world.

LAYING ON OF HANDS

The other members of the provincial council lay hands upon the provincial.

PETITION FOR BLESSING FOR THE PROVINCIAL COUNCIL

The councillors request the members' blessing, which is given in words expressive of the community's interpretation of their role.

Members: God, our Father and Mother,
    we ask you to bless these sisters.
    Guide them in their service of our congregation.
    Empower them to send us forth

in the name of Jesus and in the power of the
Spirit,
so that through us
your love may be known here on earth.

PETITION FOR BLESSING ON THE COMMUNITY

The provincial and councillors then pray over the community:

May God, the giver of all good gifts,
look upon you with love,
and bestow upon you an abundance of gifts
for the service of each other and of the Gospel.

May you live in the confidence that past blessings
awaken in your hearts,
and in the hope of the promises that God makes
to us
in the renewal of the baptismal covenant of love
and in the call to the evangelical way of life
according to the abiding example of those
who have gone before us in the community.

In all things,
may you work to the glory of God,
to whom be praise forever and ever.

All: Amen.

Concluding Rite

ALTERNATIVE 3: CELEBRATION OF THE COMPLETION OF A DIOCESAN-BASED PROGRAM OF MINISTRY TRAINING

Evelyn Eaton Whitehead and
David N. Power, O.M.I.

Those who have recently completed the ministry training program are seated in the body of the church, each among members of his or her own local community of faith.

Introductory Rites

PROCESSIONAL

WELCOME

The director of the training program welcomes all and introduces the ministers for the rite.

CALL TO PRAYER: led by director.

Liturgy of the Word

READING: 1 Sam 3:1-10 or Jer 1:4-8

READING: Gal 3:26-29 or 1 Cor 10:16-17

GOSPEL: Matt 5:1-16

HOMILY

The homily is given by a recent graduate of the training program who is now in ministry.

Renewal of Baptismal Commitment

The bishop instructs the assembly on the connections between all ministry and baptism, leads the community in a brief renewal of their baptismal commitment, and asks the community's prayers for his own ministry of service and leadership among them.

Rite of Confirmation of Ministers

Presentation of Ministers

The director of the training program calls each minister, announcing the name of his or her faith community. The minister stands in place, along with a representative of the local community. The representative makes a brief statement of the minister's area of service in the local community.

After all the ministers have been presented, the bishop presents the group to the larger assembly, leads the assembly in prayer for them, and asks the assembly to affirm their movement into ministry through applause.

Conferral of Insignia

Accompanied by a representative from the local community, each minister comes forward to receive from the bishop a sign of the completion of the program of training, for example, a certificate or pin. The bishop calls each minister by name, affirms the particular ministry to which he or she is called, and acknowledges the representative of the local community. Ministers and representatives return to their places in the body of the church.

Ministers stand at their places and recite together a "statement of mission" prepared by them as an expression of their call and goal in ministry.

A period of silence follows.

Litany of Thanksgiving

Director: Let us give thanks to God for all the gifts so freely bestowed upon us.

All: R̷. We praise you, O Lord, for all your works are wonderful.

Director: For the gifts of your Holy Spirit
sent through Jesus Christ:
for love and zeal,
for courage and wisdom. R̷.

For the Church, Christ's body,
for the call to ministry
and the grace to accept. ℟.

For the gift of each other,
for the loving care, understanding, and support
of family, friends,
mentors, teachers, colleagues. ℟.

For a future unfolding of the call we have
    answered in baptism
and for the knowledge
that your Holy Spirit will be with us. ℟.

Concluding Rite

BLESSING: The bishop leads all in a final blessing.

RECESSIONAL

ALTERNATIVE 4: CELEBRATION OF THE APPOINTMENT OF A DIRECTOR OF RELIGIOUS EDUCATION IN A PARISH

David N. Power, O.M.I.

It is envisaged that parents and other adults are responsible for the religious education of the children.

All members of the parish are invited to take part. The adults who are engaged in the work of religious education are gathered together, with the newly appointed director in their midst. The pastor presides at the service.

The Rituals

OPENING SONG: The service opens with some appropriate hymn.

GREETING

Presider: (in these or similar words)
              Today we are welcoming *N.* who has come
                  among us
              to take up the appointment as director of religious
                  education.
              We are gathered to give God thanks
              for the gifts of teaching in our parish
              and for the work that is done in the Spirit of
                  Christ
              for the education of our children.

> We ask that this work may continue to be blessed
> and that our parish may ever grow
> as a community of faith and love.

READING: Rom 12:1-8

RESPONSE: An appropriate response is chosen from the parish repertory.

GOSPEL: Matt 19:13-15

COMMITMENT OF EDUCATORS

The pastor addresses these questions to all the religious educators, who respond in unison:

Presider: In full recognition of the lordship of Jesus Christ,
and in fidelity to the gifts of the Spirit,
do you undertake the work of religious education
for the children of our parish?

Educators: We do.

Presider: Do you promise to perform this work diligently
and with due preparation,
and in a spirit of true love,
always holding the children and your
fellow-workers in high regard?

Educators: We do.

The presider then addresses these questions to the newly appointed director:

Presider: Do you wish to be a member of this parish
community,
to share its life, its joys and troubles,
so that together we may grow in the knowledge
and love of God?

Director: I do.

Presider: Do you undertake the direction of our religious
education program,
in response to the gifts of the Spirit that you
have received,
and out of a sincere desire to serve the
community,
especially through its children and its teachers?

Director: I do.

Presider: May God bless you and all your fellow-workers
in the work that you do.

PRAYER OF THANKSGIVING

Presider: God, source of all goodness,
we thank you for the continued presence of the
Risen Christ in this church,
and for the power of the Spirit
that gives us the ministries that we need
to grow to Christ's full stature.

All: May God be praised and glorified forever.

Presider: We thank you for inspiring our community
with the love of its children
and with the many endowments of the Spirit
that enable us in different ways
to enable them to grow and mature in the love of
Christ and neighbor
and to face life in a spirit of hope and service.

All: May God be praised and glorified forever.

Presider: We thank you for the dedication and love
of parents and guardians
who watch with loving care over the daily lives
of the children,
so that they may grow in happiness and
responsibility,
learning through the love of others
to come to your love.

All: May God be praised and glorified forever.

Presider: We thank you, in particular,
for the gifts of word and teaching
that are given to our educators,
and for the presence in our community
of N. (director).

All: May God be praised and glorified forever.

Presider: We ask you, O God,
to watch over this work of education,

<blockquote>
to bless the children in your great love,
and to attend and guide the work of our religious
teachers.
</blockquote>

All: Grant us, O God, your Spirit.

Presider: We ask you in a special way
to give your blessings to N.,
who has come among us to direct this work.
May she/he find here a community of love
and support,
so that our common efforts may be directed
to the glory of your name,
through Christ our Lord.

All: Amen.

Each teacher is then presented with a Bible and a manual of religious education.

A celebration of the Eucharist may follow, or the service may close with an appropriate hymn from the parish repertory.

Note: A similar service, with obvious modifications, could be held for the appointment of a music director, a director of social work, a director of youth ministry, etc.

Index